Books should be returned or renewed by the last date
above. Renew by phone **08458 247 200** or online
www.kent.gov.uk/libs

Libraries & Archives

The
ARCHAEOLOGY
of the DYKES

FROM THE ROMANS TO OFFA'S DYKE

MARK BELL

AMBERLEY

First published 2012

Amberley Publishing
The Hill, Stroud
Gloucestershire, GL5 4EP

www.amberleybooks.com

British Library Cataloguing in Publication Data.
A catalogue record for this book is available from the British Library.

ISBN 978 1 4456 0133 5

Typesetting and Origination by Amberley Publishing.
Printed in Great Britain.

CONTENTS

LIST OF ILLUSTRATIONS

LIST OF PHOTOGRAPHS

LIST OF MAPS

ACKNOWLEDGEMENTS

I would like to thank all the people who helped with this book over the years. Firstly the people at the following county historic environmental records who supplied information: Derbyshire County Council; Bath and North East Somerset Council; Berkshire Archaeology; Cambria Archaeology; the Cambridgeshire Archaeology Historic Environment Record; the Cornwall and Scilly Historic Environment Record; Dorset County Council; the Greater Manchester Archaeology Unit; the Hampshire Sites and Monuments Record; Hertfordshire County Council Historic Environment Record; Kent County Council; Leicestershire County Council; Norfolk Landscape Archaeology; Oxfordshire County Council South Yorkshire Archaeology Service; Suffolk County Council Archaeology Service; West Berkshire Sites and Monuments Record; West Yorkshire Archaeology Service Sites and Monuments Record and the Wiltshire County Council Archaeology Service. I would especially like to thank Nicholas Bodrini at North Yorkshire County Council, Isobel Thompson at Hertfordshire County Council and Jeff Spencer at Clwyd Powys Archaeological Trust who all helped above and beyond the call of duty. I would like to thank the Society of Antiquaries of London for the use of their library. I would also like to thank Dr Mark Hounslow at Lancaster University and Murray Cook at Oxford Archaeology North for providing me with unpublished reports on the Scot's Dyke. Jens Andresen at Aarhus University and Per Ethberg at the Sønderjylland museum supplied information about Denmark. I would like to thank Dr Phil Mills, Jeff Spencer and Ehren Milner for their comments on early drafts of the book and Catherine Donne and Noel Boothroyd for help with trips to various dykes. Finally I would like to thank my parents for their encouragement and support.

CHAPTER 1
INTRODUCTION

dyke (also dike)
1. a long wall or embankment built to prevent flooding, esp. from the sea.
2a. a ditch or artificial watercourse. b Brit. a natural watercourse.
3a. a low wall, esp. of turf. b a causeway.
4. a barrier or obstacle; a defence.
[Middle English from Old Norse dík or Middle Low German dik 'dam', Middle Dutch dijc 'ditch, dam': cf. ditch]

(Concise Oxford Dictionary Ninth Edition)

Across Britain there are dozens of monuments known either as ditches or dykes and formally labelled linear earthworks by archaeologists. They are a simple type of monument, made of an earth bank, usually with a ditch along one side. Some are short, only a few hundred metres in length, while others run for kilometres across the landscape; some follow a straight line across the landscape, while others trace a more winding course. These dykes have exotic names such as Bokerley Dyke, the Fleam Ditch, the Black Ditches and the Grey Ditch. There are also multiple instances of Grim's Ditch, Grim's Dyke and Devil's Dyke across the country. The largest of these dykes, Wansdyke and Offa's Dyke, are comparable in scale to Roman monuments such as Hadrian's Wall and the Antonine Wall. Their origins and purpose have been a source of argument since the antiquarians first described them.

These monuments have different names in different parts of the country. While Ditch or Dyke is common the term Rig or Ridge is also used. It is unfortunate that the term *dyke* can also refer to a Roman road such as the Ackling Dyke in Wiltshire. The raised bank of earth that formed the base of a Roman road, known as an *agger*, has sometimes been mistaken for a dyke and dykes have been confused with Roman roads. Linear earthwork is an unwieldy but more neutral term. For consistency I have tried to use the term dyke throughout this book.

This book aims to examine the dykes that date to the period after the end of Roman power in Britain, the time known as the Dark Ages, or the early medieval period. There

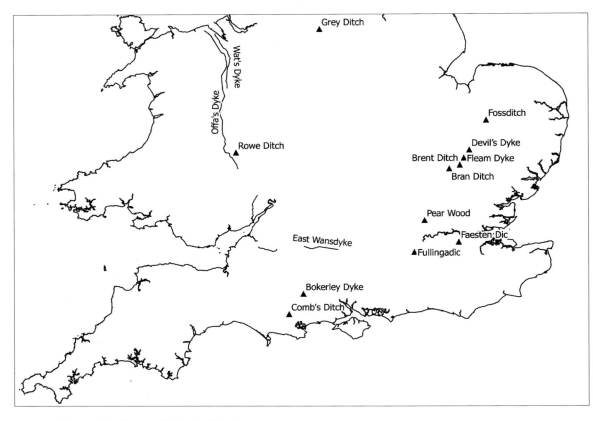

Map 1: Post-Roman Dykes in Britain.

is some confusion between these post-Roman dykes and the similar linear earthworks of prehistoric, mainly Iron Age, date. While some dykes definitely belong to the Iron Age and others are certainly post-Roman, the dating of many is still uncertain. Many monuments, once assigned to the post-Roman period, are now known to be definitely prehistoric after excavation; while others have been assigned to the prehistoric period on the basis of very little evidence. A good example is the Chiltern Grim's Ditch, once thought to be post-Roman, and now recognised to be a complex of Iron Age monuments (J. F. Dyer). Further confusion is caused by the reuse of prehistoric dykes in the post-Roman period, such as the Aves Ditch in Oxfordshire. Even when a monument like Offa's Dyke, is linked with an historic person – Offa, King of Mercia, from AD 757 to 796 – the evidence that it was built by King Offa of Mercia is not as clear and unambiguous as once assumed. Even the evidence for the extent of Offa's dyke has recently been the subject of academic debate.

Most of the questions about the dykes remain unanswered despite several hundred years of fieldwork and observation by archaeologists and antiquarians. When exactly were they built? Why were they built? Who built them? How did they function? For most of the dykes we still do not know their original extent or whether the gaps in them were original or cut through at a later date.

Map 2: Dykes of prehistoric date in Britain.

The aim of this book is to summarise what we do know about the dykes, and to speculate about what we don't know. A brief discussion of some of the history of work on the dykes and the theoretical beliefs of the archaeologists who pioneered studies of the dykes is needed followed by a survey of the dykes region by region. The question of who built the dykes needs a very brief outline of late Roman and post-Roman archaeology and how the dykes fit into what we think we know about these periods. The final part is a discussion of how the dykes could have functioned, possible reasons why they were built, and how they may have fitted into the post-Roman landscape.

The dykes in their historic and archaeological context, as part of post-Roman Britain, are a neglected area of study. There has been a kind of benign neglect since death of O. G. S. Crawford in the 1950s. That is not to say that individual

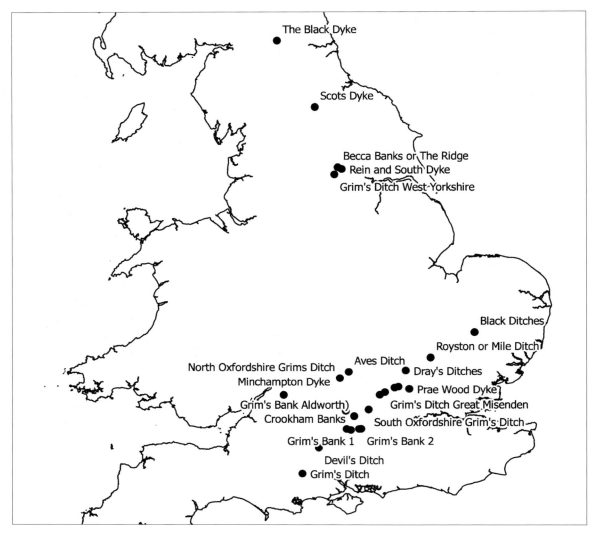

Map 3: Dykes of unknown date in Britain.

monuments have been neglected but study of the dykes as a group. Much has been written and published on individual monuments, mostly in local archaeological journals but there has not been a survey of the dykes as a whole. In the last few years there has been a boom in books about the end of Roman Britain and the post-Roman period, as the 1,600th anniversary of the traditional end of Roman Britain has approached. Most of these books mentioned the dykes but in a superficial way with little discussion of how the most substantial monuments of post-Roman Britain fit into this period.

Why have the dykes been neglected? Part of the problem is that current debates about the post-Roman period concentrate on ethnicity, 'Celtic' survival and how long a Roman-style economy persisted after the end of Roman political power. The fifth and sixth centuries are divided between those scholars who see the period as an ending, a decline and fall of Roman Britain, and those who see it as a beginning, the start of England and Englishness. The dykes don't quite fit into the current view of a slow and relatively peaceful transformation of dress and jewellery styles. An earlier generation of archaeologists who saw the change of Roman Britain to Anglo-Saxon England as a violent invasion by a Germanic race overcoming a Celtic one, had less of a problem with the construction of large defensive earthworks.

Another problem is that the dykes are both simple constructions but difficult to interpret. It seems unlikely that they were permanently manned fortifications. Were the dykes more symbolic monuments than defensive fortifications? If they were defences how could they be used either tactically or strategically? No certain mention of any of the dykes is to be found in any of the small number of historic sources we have for this period. There may be allusions to dykes in some of the historic sources but nothing is clear.

There is still much myth and misinformation about the dykes and confusion about individual dykes, some monuments once thought to be post-Roman are now known to be Iron Age but the old dates persist in the literature. Some of the ideas about the dykes are ideas about the dykes fossilised in the 1930s. As late as 1983 the idea of the Chiltern Grim's Ditch being the northern boundary of post-Roman London was still being suggested (Merrifield) and the idea of a post-Roman dyke all around Galloway is still mentioned occasionally (Grigg).

The term the 'Dark Ages' has also gone out of fashion, and the period AD 410 to AD 700 is covered by a number of labels such as the post-Roman period, sub-Roman period, early medieval period or early Anglo-Saxon period depending on your point of view.

Antiquarianism and the Dykes

Interest in the dykes goes back to the very beginnings of British archaeology in the writings of antiquarians such as John Leland and William Stukeley. The dykes were conspicuous monuments in the landscape and had obviously required much effort and labour to build. Who built them soon became a matter of debate as antiquarians tried to fit them into their knowledge of the ancient world. There was a major debate on whether the dykes were built before or after the Roman period. For William Stukeley the Wansdyke, as so much else was definitely a Belgic (prehistoric) work:

> There is a very plain reason: that Stonehenge was built, before the Wandike was made, and that was the last boundary of the Belgic kingdom in Britain. The stones of which Stonehenge is compos'd, were fetcht from beyond that boundary, consequently then an enemies country. It seems not improbable, that the Wansdike was made, when this Belgic kingdom was at its height, and that time we may well guess at, from Cæsar.

Belgic or Saxon Works?

Other antiquarians such as the Revd J. Goldsmith believed the dykes were definitely Saxon works:

> A little to the south-west of Savernake Forest, is a famous Saxon monument, Called Wansdyke, which runs across the country from east to west. The name Wansdyke is a corruption of Woden's Dyke, or ditch; so called from Woden, one of the deities of the Pagan Saxons. The most probable opinion concerning this fortification is, that it was thrown up by the first king of the west Saxons, to check the continual incursions of the Britons, who continued for many years to attempt the recovery of their ancient liberty. It is a string earthen rampart with a broad ditch on the south, and may be traced in Bath in Somersetshire to Great Bedwin in Wiltshire.

Some like J. Norris Brewer were uncertain about the date of the dyke and tried to have it both ways:

> The most stupendous of these ancient boundary lines is that called Wansdike, which is 80 miles in length, and is still visible for than three parts of that extent. This deep ditch and lofty vallum, are supposed to have formed the line of demarkation between the Belgæ and the aboriginal Britons, although afterwards in part adopted by the Anglo-Saxons.

Edwin Guest (1800–80) was the first person to go out and seriously examine monuments in the field. His papers were published posthumously as the *Origines Celticae* (Guest). As the *Dictionary of National Biography* says, 'The Origines itself is a fragmentary, lengthy, and largely unread treatise on a deeply perplexing theme'. Guest firmly believed all the dykes and earthworks were the work of the Belgae. Other archaeologists such as General Pitt Rivers in *Excavations in Bokerly and Wansdyke Dorset and Wilts 1888 – 1891*, were not prepared to be so certain without more evidence:

> Dr Guest, in his well-known paper on what he terms 'the Belgic Ditches' appears to me to be perfectly right in assuming that these continuous entrenchments must necessarily have been the work of a people in a higher condition of civilization, to secure their territory against the depredations of an inferior people, in a lower condition of life. But, whether he is right in adopting Stukeley's opinion that these superior people were Belgæ, is a question which I am not prepared, either to accept or deny, without better evidence.

Pitt Rivers was the first to use excavation to answer questions about the dykes and to investigate them methodically. So excavations of the dykes were part of the birth of modern scientific archaeology. As a large land owner Pitt Rivers fortunately had the time and money to carry out his excavations and also a slice of luck.

Scientific investigation of the dykes began with a church organist and a farmer. One day in the middle of 1888, a Mr Lawes, who was the church organist of Tollard Royal in Wiltshire, was travelling past the hamlet of Woodyates, on the borders of Wiltshire, Dorset and Hampshire, close to the earthwork known as Bokerly or Bokerley Dyke. There he saw a farmer digging away part of the Dyke, to use the material for fertiliser for his fields. Fortunately Mr Lawes was also employed as the conductor of the band set up by a local landowner, who happened to be General Pitt Rivers. As the General was well known for his interest in archaeology Mr Lawes brought him some coins and a fibula from the diggings. Pitt Rivers knew that this was an opportunity for him to answer the question about the date of Bokerley Dyke. Was this dyke built during the prehistoric, Roman or post-Roman periods? As Pitt Rivers wrote later 'so at once I applied to Sir Edward Hulse, the owner of the property, who readily gave me permission to dig a section through the rampart at this spot ...' (Pitt Rivers, *Excavations in Bokerly and Wansdyke Dorset and Wilts 1888 – 1891*)

The results showed that Bokerley Dyke had a least two phases and the ditch of the dyke was cut thorough the Roman road, blocking the roadway. Then after some time the ditch was filled in and the road reopened. A second and longer lasting blocking of the road took place sometime later when the ditch was re-cut. Pitt Rivers proved to his satisfaction that Bokerley Dyke must have been built in the late Roman or early post-Roman period.

Soon after the Bokerley Dyke excavations Pitt Rivers had an opportunity to examine another of the dykes in what sound like ideal excavation conditions.

The investigations in Bokerly Dyke were not far advanced, when on the 2nd of June, 1888, I received a letter from the Rev. A. C. Smith ... urging me to undertake the excavation of Wansdyke ... I commenced operations on April 2nd, 1889, working until April 17th, and after an interval of a year and a quarter, renewed them on July 28th, 1890, at the time of the meeting of the Wilts Archæological Society at Devizes. I took up my quarters at the 'Bear', at Devizes, driving up the hill every morning, so as to arrive at the time the men commenced work, and returning every evening after the work was over.

(Pitt Rivers, *Excavations in Bokerly and Wansdyke Dorset and Wilts 1888 – 1891*)

The results were equally satisfactory. Pitt Rivers found that the bank of the Wansdyke was built over layers containing coarse Romano-British pottery and artefacts as well as having Romano-British pottery in the bank and filling of the ditch. Another section of the bank sealed a Romano-British enclosure. This showed that the Wansdyke could not have been built before the Roman period.

The Early Twentieth Century

The dykes attracted the attention of several major twentieth-century archaeologists. Their work has had a continuing influence on the interpretation and understanding of the dykes up to the present day. Probably the most influential of all the archaeologists who investigated the dykes was O. G. S. Crawford.

Osbert Guy Stanhope Crawford (1886–1957) spent most of his archaeological career at the Ordnance Survey where he was responsible for adding and correcting details of archaeological monuments on Ordnance Survey maps. Crawford was also a pioneer of aerial photography, a pioneer of using a geographic approach to archaeology and of popularising archaeology through his editorship of the journal *Antiquity*. It is difficult to underestimate the importance of Crawford to the development of British archaeology in the first half of the twentieth century. Crawford proudly called himself a 'field archaeologist', meaning someone who observes and surveys, and after he joined the Ordnance Survey, he did no excavation work. Also Crawford could be over-enthusiastic, and he assigned many dykes to the post-Roman period on typological comparison with other earthworks of similar type which became a circular argument. The only evidence for the date of many earthworks turns out to be Crawford's opinion, for example, those in Cornwall. While at the Ordnance Survey Crawford was responsible for a series of period maps such as *Roman Britain* and *Britain in the Dark Ages*. The Dark Age map was first produced in two sheets; south and then north (Ordnance Survey), which was the first map to show the distribution of post-Roman dykes.

The other figure who did important work on the study of the dykes was Sir Cyril Fox (1882–1967). Like Crawford, Cyril Fox took a geographical approach to archaeology and pioneered the use of the distribution map. His first major work was on the archaeology of the Cambridge region (C. Fox, *The Archaeology of the Cambridge Region*) where he showed the Cambridgeshire Dykes were most likely to be post-Roman in date. Between 1925 and 1932 he excavated on Offa's Dyke publishing the results as a series of papers in *Archaeologica Cambrensis*, and was published in book form in 1955 (C. Fox, *Offa's Dyke*). He also did a major survey of the Wansdyke with his wife Aileen in the 1950s (Fox & Fox). Another of his major works was called *The Personality of Britain* where Fox was the first to divide Britain into a Highland and a Lowland zone, based on geology and climate.

Unfortunately both Crawford and Fox were working under a set of assumptions about the landscape and environment of prehistoric Britain that has now been superseded. These assumptions constrained their interpretation of the dykes. The first major belief was about the environment of prehistoric and Roman Britain. This was that low-lying river valleys and heavy soils were covered with thick impenetrable primeval oak forests that could not have been cleared by prehistoric peoples, using primitive stone tools. The major foci of settlement had to be on the lighter chalk soils of the downs of lowland Britain and clay and other heavy soils were not cultivated until the medieval period, when heavier ploughs became available. This is what Crawford called the '*Archaic*' period of agriculture, from the Neolithic to early medieval times where prehistoric and Roman settlement stuck close to the lighter chalk and sandy soils.

All movement of people and of material culture was therefore along the narrow strips of land that connected the areas of chalk. Salisbury Plain and the Cotswolds were seen as the central meeting point between 'Atlantic' and continental influences.

Fox takes it as axiomatic that population was concentrated on these lighter chalk soils and in a startling quote he dismisses any settlement not on the chalk of the lowlands:

> All human communities, of course, throw off groups and families below the poverty line of their particular culture, who scratch a miserable living how they can in the less desirable areas. Evidence of such will certainly be found from time to time on the clays of the Lowland; but they are negligible.
>
> (C. Fox, *The Personality of Britain*)

In the second half of the twentieth century two major technological innovations changed this picture completely. The use of large scale and systematic programmes of aerial photography, of which O. G. S. Crawford had been a pioneer, showed that settlement on the gravels and clays of the lowlands were as dense as on the chalk soils. The pattern of upstanding earthworks was a result of differential survival. The lighter soils were mainly used for pasture after the prehistoric period and were not ploughed, preserving the earthworks while any monuments on heavier soils were not likely to have survived as upstanding remains due to repeated ploughing over thousands of years.

The second technological innovation was the use of palynology (pollen analysis) to reconstruct the past environment of Britain. This showed that the thick primeval forests of southern Britain were mostly cleared away by the Neolithic period. The landscape would have had more woodland and scrub than today but would not have been the impassable 'damp oakwood' that Crawford and Fox believed.

This idea of the impassable wooded landscape created another idea about the landscape of Britain which still lingers on today. To explain the distribution of artefacts, whether Neolithic axes or Bronze Age hoards, long distance trade routes would have been needed to go round this impenetrable forest. Travel across the lowland zone must have used paths along the high chalk downs, the so-called 'Ridgeways' that connected the areas of lighter soils together.

The existence of such long distance routes is still generally accepted without question despite the dramatically changed view of the prehistoric environment and of prehistoric social organisation since the work done by Crawford and Fox. The idea of such 'ridgeways' has proved to be an enduring archaeological myth and one prominent archaeologist Andrew Sherratt once called them a fashionable version of ley lines.

Because the ridgeways are always assumed to have existed in most discussion about the dykes it is necessary to describe them. In *Archaeology in the Field*, Crawford defined four main long distance tracks of prehistoric date. They are the South Downs Ridgeway, the North Downs Ridgeway, the Icknield Way and the Jurassic Way. According to Crawford, the South Downs Ridgeway starts near Beachy Head and proceeds to Winchester where 'west of Winchester there is no single track that could be called its continuation'. The North Downs track follows the escarpment of the

North Downs where the eastern part is referred to as the Pilgrim's Way. The western part of the North Downs Ridgeway proceeds from Basingstoke and runs along the Hog's Back and is called the Harroway once it enters Hampshire. It goes on to Stonehenge and 'we may think of it re-appearing in Devon and Cornwall'.

Crawford's route for the Icknield Way starts in Norfolk on the Wash and he takes it through Thetford and into Cambridgeshire. On the Cambridgeshire section of the Icknield Way Crawford wrote, 'Through Cambridgeshire its existence is proved not only by medieval references to the existing trackway but also by the great dykes which bar its course.'

Here Crawford uses the presence of dykes to prove the existence of the trackway; unfortunately this became a circular argument that relied on the existence of the Icknield Way to provide the need for the dykes to block it. The route of the Icknield Way then follows the Chilterns through Luton and Dunstable to the Thames. The Chiltern escarpment is protected by the Chiltern Grim's Ditch which was also believed by Crawford to be post-Roman in date (see Appendix for more on the existence of the Chiltern Grim's Ditch). At the Thames Crawford split the Icknield Way in two and had the lower branch do a strange loop, crossing the Thames at Goring and turning north to Wantage and then meeting the northern branch again at West Kennett. Meanwhile the northern branch crosses the Thames at Pangborne and carries on to Aldworth where it is barred by the Aldworth Dyke. Crawford then takes the Icknield Way into the Berkshire Ridgeway for a meeting near Stonehenge with the other trackways at the Longbarrow Crossroads on Salisbury Plain.

Crawford's final long distance route is the Jurassic Way running from the Humber to the Bristol Avon. Again the presence of a dyke is used to mark its route 'southwest of Grantham we may get a hint of its course from King Lud's Bank on Saltby Heath ... ' King Lud's Entrenchment is another potential post-Roman dyke, on the boundary between Leicestershire and Lincolnshire, used to indicate the existence of the route.

The existence of the Jurassic Way as a defined long distance route was shown to be untenable by Christopher Taylor in 1979 (Taylor, *Roads and Tracks of Britain*). The Jurassic Way was another artefact of the poorly known distribution of sites and monuments in Crawford's time. Modern distribution maps show no special concentration of sites and monuments along the supposed route of the Jurassic Way.

Recent work has also cast doubt on the existence of the Icknield Way as a long distance highway (Harrison). The first mention of the Icknield Way as a long distance road goes back to Henry of Huntingdon in the twelfth century as one of the four highways of Britain.

Britain was so dear to its inhabitants that they constructed four highways in it: from one end to the other, built by royal authority, so that no one would dare to attack an enemy on them. The first is from east to west, and is called the Icknield Way. The second runs from south to north and is called Ermine Street. The third goes across from Dover to Chester, that is from the southeast to the northwest, and is called Watling Street. The fourth, longer than the others, begins in Caithness and ends in Totnes that is from the beginning of Cornwall to the end of Scotland. This road is called the Fosse Way, takes a diagonal route from southwest to northeast and paces through Lincoln.

(Henry of Huntingdon, *Historia Anglorum*)

It has been suggested that Henry made the number of roads up to four because of the mystical properties of four. The other three highways are all Roman roads and Henry is explicit in stating the starting and finishing point of each while the Icknield Way just runs east to west. Eighteenth- and nineteenth-century antiquarians tried to define the precise course of the Icknield Way but could not agree on the exact route. Gradually it would be accepted by archaeologists that the Icknield Way was a 'zone of communication' with no precise route. It was seen as a natural highway along the scarp of the Chilterns from a hundred yards to a mile wide. The course of the Icknield Way could only be seen by the concentration of visible prehistoric monuments such as barrows marking the way. Once the heavy clay soils were seen to be as densely settled as the lighter chalk soils, the appearance of the Icknield Way could be seen as yet another artifact of differential preservation. The chalk escarpment of the Chilterns was heavily used in prehistoric times, enough to cause major soil degradation. Subsequently the land could only be used for pasture. This had the fortunate effect of preserving the prehistoric features on the escarpment from the plough. There does not seem to be room for a long-distance highway along the Chiltern escarpment, through a landscape filled with field boundaries, and with ditches and dykes built as agricultural land boundaries, not for defence.

As anthropological models have become more common in archaeology the existence of long-distance traders and the need for such long-distance trade routes has been questioned. Trade is now seen as a much more socially embedded activity, used as part of a gift-giving culture. There is no need for long distance paths to explain the distribution of goods such as Neolithic axes. Short distance exchange, called 'down the line' trade can explain the distribution maps.

In examining the evidence for the Icknield Way, Harrison has shown that Anglo-Saxon place name evidence only refers to five places between Wanborough in Wiltshire and Risborough in Buckinghamshire. There are other place names with the element 'Ick-' but many do not lie on the supposed route of the Icknield Way and may either come from the Anglo-Saxon personal name 'Icel/Icca' or refer to the presence of a British church. 'The Icknield Way is one of the last bastions of the traditional archaeology, in which prehistoric activity is confined to lighter land and "trade" means much the same as now.' (Harrison)

The Icknield Way can now be seen as a short roadway of Anglo-Saxon date, not a long distance prehistoric superhighway. Unfortunately many discussions of the dykes still refer to them as blocking or controlling movement along routes such as the Icknield Way or other long distance trackways.

Changing Views of Post-Roman Britain

In AD 400 most of Britain was a normal if troubled part of the Roman Empire. Roman rule had lasted for 350 years and a large part of the Roman army was based in the northern part of Britain. By the time of St Augustine's arrival in Kent in AD 598 Britain was divided into a number of small kingdoms, pagan and Germanic-speaking in the south and east and Christian and Celtic-speaking in the north, west and south-west.

In AD 410 the emperor Honorius wrote to the cities of Britain saying they should look after their own defences. After this Britain never, as far as we know, came back under Roman political control. Up to the 1970s it was generally accepted that Romano-British society survived beyond AD 410 into the fifth century with 'business as usual' until destroyed by the mass invasions and settlement of Angles, Saxons and Jutes. It was expected that the expansion of rescue archaeology would soon find evidence of fifth-century town life, for example Martin Biddle in *The Future of London's Past* confidently predicted that 'London would have been unusual in south-eastern Britain if it were not still in some sense an organized community as late as AD 440-50'.

Since the 1970s there has been a radical change in our view of late and post-Roman Britain. Towns in Britain seem to have economically collapsed well before the end of the Roman. There are conflicting views of late Roman Britain. Some have seen the late Roman period as a period of long slow decline, for example, Neil Faulkner. Faulkner is a proponent of the view that Roman Britain ended in decay and squalor, the result of a natural process of decay. Others, concentrating on the west of the province have seen the fourth century as 'The Golden Age of Roman Britain' (de la Bédoyère), where the collapse of Roman political control in the fifth century is sudden and unexpected. Yet a third view had been put forward by Ken Dark (Dark). Dark, concentrating on the South West and Wales sees the end of Roman Britain as parallel to the transformation that occurred in the rest of the Roman world. The west of Britain becomes transformed into a 'Late Antique' society, which is in close contact with the society of the late Roman Mediterranean.

There has also been a change in how the Anglo-Saxon settlement occurred. The Anglo-Saxon settlement is now seen as a minor event, at least in terms of numbers:

> The general trend at present is to believe that Germanic settlement by immigrants was gradual, fragmented into small groups, and relatively peaceful, the newcomers either setting up in under-utilised land or integrating themselves into the existing fifth or sixth century settlements.
>
> (P. Rahtz)

Some have argued that a very small number of Germanic immigrants arrived (Pryor), and there was a gradual change from Roman-British to Anglo-Saxon identity as the native population adopted new styles of dress and ornament.

We do not know exactly how long Romanised society survived in Britain after AD 410. The crucial problem is one of dating of archaeological sites. Once the Roman army was withdrawn from Britain the supply of new coins to the province of ceased. How long a monetary economy lasted and coins continued to circulate is unknown and dating of sites from coin evidence becomes impossible. Also pottery production on a large scale ended as well, either due to collapse of the monetary economy or because the major customer, the army had left Britain. This makes it impossible to date the end of archaeological sites with any accuracy. Some have seen a Romanised lifestyle ending by AD 420 while others have tried to push the ending of a Roman lifestyle in Britain down to AD 450 or AD 480.

The question is where the dykes fit into this transformation of Roman Britain into Anglo-Saxon England? Offa's Dyke is seen as a frontier between the English and the Welsh but did the other dykes 'mark stages of conflict between Celts and Anglo-Saxons' or did they mark Romano-British territories or early Saxon kingdoms?

CHAPTER 2
REGIONAL SURVEY

But by far the best was the map of "Britain in the Dark Ages", in two sheets (North and South). I put some of my best work into this and so did Curtis, and I regard it as the best thing produced so far by the Archaeological Branch of the Ordnance Survey.

(O. G. Crawford, *Said and Done: The Autobiography of an Archaeologist*)

The starting point for any survey of the potential post-Roman dykes has to be the Dark Age maps published by the Ordnance Survey in 1935 and 1966. O. G. S. Crawford's list of post-Roman dykes from the 1935 map is shown in table 1.

Name	Location (1935 county)
Heydon Ditch	Cambridgeshire
Fleam Ditch	Cambridgeshire
Devils Ditch	Cambridgeshire
Bolster Bank	Cornwall
The Giant's Hedge	Cornwall
Grey Ditch	Derbyshire
Bokerly Dyke	Dorset
Combs Ditch	Dorset
Devil's Ditch	Hampshire near Andover
Faesten Dic	Kent
Nico Ditch	Lancashire

King Lud's Bank	Leicestershire
Foss Ditch	Norfolk
Bitcham Ditch	Norfolk
Devil's Ditch	Norfolk
Black Ditches	Suffolk
Roman Ridge	Yorkshire West Riding
Roman Rig	Yorkshire West Riding
Becca Banks	Yorkshire West Riding
Scots Dyke	Yorkshire North Riding
Chiltern Grim's Ditch	Shown as three sections
Wodnes Dic	The west Wansdyke in Somerset
Wodnes Dic	The east Wansdyke in Wiltshire
Clywd Wade	Wat's dyke
Offa's Dyke	

There are some errors and omissions from this list. The fourth Cambridgeshire dyke, known as the Brent Ditch, is not shown. Only one of the Aberford dykes, Becca Banks, is shown. The Roman Ridge (not to be confused with the Roman Ridge near Sheffield) in West Yorkshire is shown as a dyke, but it is now known to be a Roman road. The Grim's Ditch in Wychwood (the north Oxfordshire Grim's Ditch, now known to be Iron Age) was known but not included as 'it seemed to belong to a period when Roman culture was still in being'.

It is interesting that there are no Roman roads marked on this first edition of the map, except for the road from Canterbury to London. Only the ridge ways are shown as long distance routes, completely ignoring the extensive network of Roman roads which still survived in the post-Roman landscape. Even if they were not in good repair these roads would have provided the easiest route through the landscape of post-Roman Britain.

It is difficult to get a clear view of Crawford's ideas about the dykes as the only evidence left to us is the Dark Age map and the brief notes published in *Archaeology in the Field* but it seems Crawford believed that some of the post-Roman dykes, around Bedwyn and Silchester, were built by surviving British communities into late fifth century. The cover of the south sheet of the Dark Age map shows a group of Saxons attacking a walled town.

A second and revised edition of the Dark Age map was published in 1966. The notes for the map were compiled by C. W. Philips and are less certain about the dates of some dykes than Crawford's notes of the 1930s but still definitely state that 'the most impressive monuments of the Dark Ages in Britain are the great linear earthworks which define boundaries and mark stages of conflict between Celts and Anglo-Saxons as well as episodes in the internecine wars of the Kings of the Heptarchy'. (Ordnance Survey)

The actual date of some of the earthworks were in now in doubt but were included on the map:

> In some cases the Dark Age date of linear earthworks is in no doubt where they are firmly associated with historical personalities and events, or have been shown to belong to this period by excavation. Others are less certain, but where their general character and tactical design suggest a Dark Age date they have been shown on the map.

In addition there was an attempt to divide the dykes into Celtic and Anglo-Saxon works. The map showed dykes that were coloured blue for Celt works and black for Anglo-Saxon ones.

The list of earthworks from the 1966 map is:

Celtic Dykes

Name	Location
Bolster Bank	Cornwall
Giant's Hedge	Cornwall
Bokerly Ditch	Dorset
Combs Ditch	Dorset
Nico Ditch	Lancashire
Ponter's Ball	Somerset
Becca Banks	Yorkshire West Riding
Roman Rig	Yorkshire West Riding
Roman Rig	Or Roman Ridge in Yorkshire West Riding (only two of the three branches are shown)

Anglo-Saxon Dykes

Name	Location
Devil's Ditch	Cambridgeshire
Fleam Ditch	Cambridgeshire
Heydon Ditch	Cambridgeshire
Grey Ditch	Derbyshire
Faesten Dic	Kent
Rowe Ditch	Herefordshire
King Lud's Bank	Leicestershire
Launditch	Norfolk
Bichamditch	Norfolk, ditch shown on west of the dyke, not on the east
Foss Ditch	Norfolk
Devil's Ditch	Norfolk
Black Ditches	Suffolk
Dane's Dyke	Yorkshire North Riding
Scot's Dyke	North Yorkshire
Wodnes Dic	(The Wansdyke east and west sections)
Offediche (Offa's Dyke)	
Claywdd Wade (Wat's Dyke)	
Welsh Short Dykes	The Wantern Dycher and Double Deyche

Again only three of the Cambridgeshire Dykes are shown though all four are mentioned in the text. The spurious Roman Rig in West Yorkshire is still shown. The notes to the map put King Lud's Entrenchment in Leicestershire, the Scot's Dyke near Richmond, North Yorkshire, the Nico Ditch in Manchester, Comb's Ditch, the Giant's Hedge and the Bolster Bank on to the uncertain list. The Chiltern Grim's Ditch is not shown at all. While some of the Welsh short dykes are shown, linear earthworks in Scotland are omitted. The Roman road network and the Antonine Wall and Hadrian's Wall are shown on the map.

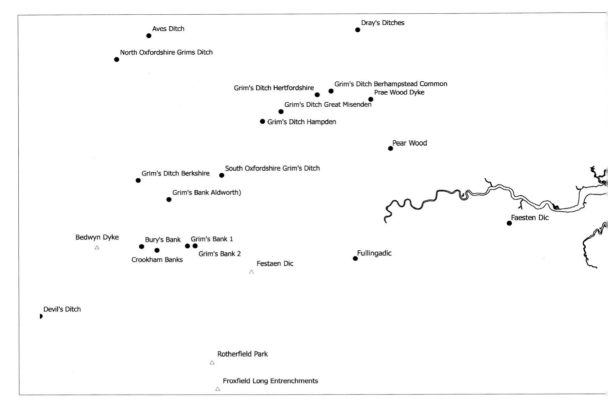

Map 4: Dykes in South East England.

Since the Ordnance Survey published the Dark Age maps, there have been many excavations and publications on individual dykes. Some dykes such as the Chiltern Grim's Ditch are certainly prehistoric while other dykes have been suggested as post-Roman. In an attempt get a list of post-Roman dykes I will survey the evidence region by region across England and Wales.

The South East: Greater London and Kent

The Middlesex Grim's Dyke

There are two separate monuments in the old county of Middlesex (now Greater London) that both Crawford and Wheeler considered part of the Chiltern Grim's Ditch system. One monument is the earthwork that runs from Pinner to Harrow Weald Common and is known as the Grim's Dyke, and the second is the earthwork in Pear Wood, Pinner that may be a continuation of the Grim's Ditch. About 8 km long, the Grim's Ditch has been badly damaged by housing development along its length. Excavations by the Inner London Archaeological Unit at the Harrow end of the Grim's Ditch (Ellis) found two very badly worn sherds of Iron Age pottery in the bank

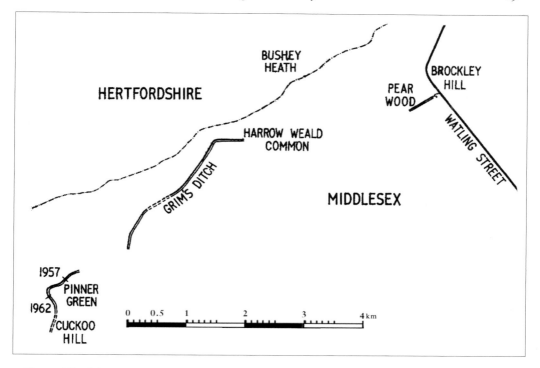

Map 5: The dykes on Harrow Weald Common and in Pear Wood after Castle, 1975.

which was a single phase of construction. A single radiocarbon date of 50 +/- 80 AD was obtained from charcoal from a heath in the bank. Calibrated this gives a calendar age of cal AD: 110 ± 94 (using CalPal http://www.calpal-online.de/).

The Pinner Grim's Ditch in Pear Wood may be the eastern end of the Middlesex Grim's Ditch or it may be a separate monument. The monument is called 'Grymesdich' in a document of AD 1535. The Pear Wood earthwork runs at a right angle to Watling Street, the main Roman road between London and St Albans. The earthwork does not go right up to Watling Street ending about 180 m to the west of Watling Street, and there is no evidence of any continuation on the east side of Watling Street. The earthwork is about 27 m wide, and the ditch is V-shaped, 4 m wide and 1.5 to 1.8 m deep. The bank is on the north side with a small counter bank on the south side. The north bank is much bigger than the ditch, suggesting material was brought in from outside to build up the bank. The dimensions are similar to the Middlesex Grim's Ditch. Several campaigns of excavation have taken place on this dyke, in 1948 and 1949, in 1954, 1955 and 1956 and finally in 1973. Finds included Iron Age and Roman pottery from the silting of the ditch. The 1955 excavation found an iron spearhead that is likely to be of Roman date though it could be possibly be of Saxon date. The ditch was lined with tile and used as a culvert in the eighteenth century. The 1973 excavations (Castle) found Roman coarse pottery recovered from the bank, including a third- or fourth-century black burnished platter and a fourth-century colour-coated beaker. No early Saxon or medieval material has been found, suggesting but not proving a late Roman or post-Roman date for the dyke.

The relationship between the two dykes is crucial. They may once have formed a continuous earthwork built as a post-Roman boundary. Alternatively there may be two separate monuments, one a long Iron Age dyke, near to, but unconnected with a smaller monument built in the late or post-Roman period to control movement along the Roman road between London and St Albans. A third possibility is that the Grim's Ditch was an Iron Age earthwork refurbished and extended in the post-Roman period. There is a small Roman settlement nearby on Brockley Hill, which may be the place referred to as *Sulloniacae* in the Antonine Itinerary. The Harrow area seems to be free of Saxon material culture for two centuries after the end of Roman Britain (Thompson, 'Harrow AD 400–AD 1066'). The Doomsday book records massive amounts of woodland in north-east Middlesex and south-west Hertfordshire, suggesting a sparse population. The Anglo-Saxons who called themselves the *Wæclingas* settled at Verulanium – hence its Anglo-Saxon name of *Watlingchester* and the name of Watling Street, while Harrow comes from the shrine of the *Gumeningas*, suggesting a pagan shrine on top of Harrow Hill. Isobel Thompson suggests that the whole Grim's Ditch was one single monument and that it was not big enough to be a defence but was a boundary marker instead either between the Anglo-Saxons or the Roman-British of London and St Albans.

Recent excavations (Bowlt) have taken place at Manor Farm Ruislip, on a possible southern extension to Grim's Dyke. The Ruislip earthwork is massive and to no obvious purpose. It was built after the second century AD as Roman sherds of this date were found in the bank. Similar in size to Grim's Dyke and the Pear Wood structure it strengthens the case for all the detached sections of dyke to form a single monument of post-Roman date.

Faestendic

The *Faestendic* stands in Joyden's Wood, near Bexley, between the valleys of the River Cray and the River Darenth. The ditch roughly follows the boundary between the modern London borough of Bexley and the county of Kent. The wood contains a number of other earthworks of unknown date. The dyke has been identified with the one mentioned in an Anglo-Saxon charter of AD 814 which describes the boundaries of Bexley, where it is referred to as the *faestendic*. *Faestendic* has been translated as fortress dyke or strong dyke. The *Faestendic* is a scheduled ancient monument but the scheduled area covers only a part of the original earthwork. Old Ordnance Survey maps show it extending to the north, an area that has since been destroyed by housing development. We know that the dyke must date before AD 814 and excavation has shown the bank contains pottery that dates not before 100 BC. (H. A. Hogg)

The *Faestendic* probably, though not certainly, extended further north where it would intersect the Roman road from Canterbury to London, Watling Street, the line of which is followed by the modern A2.

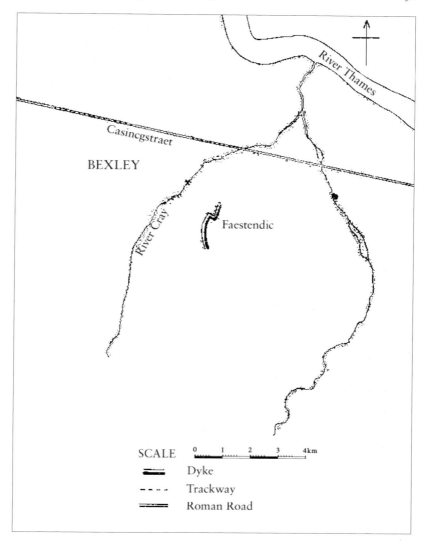

Map 6: The
Faestendic near
Bexley in Kent.

Several other *Faestendic*s are known – this name has been applied to part of
the Chiltern Grim's Ditch, the dyke on Hartford Bridge flats (A. H. Hogg), and to
the Devil's Ditch near Andover. Hogg (H. A. Hogg) has pointed out that the Kent
Faestendic separates the Cray and Darenth valleys. While Roman remains are equally
common in both valleys early Anglo-Saxon remains are confined to the Darenth
valley. The dyke faces westwards towards the Cray valley so Hogg suggests this
was an Anglo-Saxon boundary marker. Attempts to link this dyke to the battle of
Crecganford (Crayford) in AD 457 can only be speculation as there is no real dating
evidence for the *Faestendic*. If the *Faestendic* really did extend to Watling Street then
the dyke would be ideally sited to control movement eastwards along the Roman road
towards Canterbury and would strengthen the case for it being post-Roman.

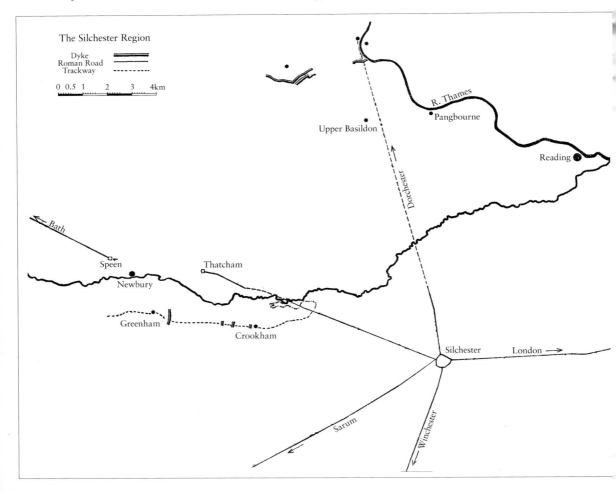

Map 7: Dykes in the Silchester region.

The South: Berkshire and Hampshire

The Silchester Dykes

The concept of the Silchester Dykes was defined by B. H. St J. O'Neil in an article in *Antiquity* in 1944 (O'Neil, 'The Silchester Region in the 5th & 6th centuries AD'). The town of Silchester has been suggested as a Romano-British enclave that persisted into the fifth century despite being surrounded by Anglo-Saxon settlement. The modern county boundary kinks around Silchester, possibly preserving an ancient boundary. Silchester is in Hampshire while the dykes are just across the county boundary in Berkshire.

It is important to remember that O'Neill proceeded from the assumption that Silchester was occupied in the fifth century and therefore the dykes were needed for protection, not the other way round. Subsequently the existence of the Silchester Dykes has been used to 'prove' continuing occupation into the fifth century.

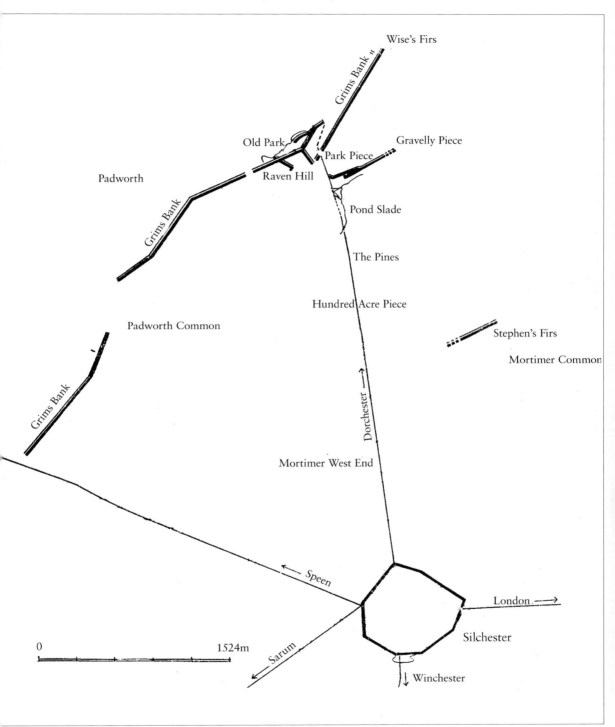

Map 8: The Silchester dykes.

There are at least four sets of earthworks around Silchester that could belong to the post-Roman period, but none have firm dating evidence. All are short lengths of earthwork and relate to tracks or Roman roads.

O'Neil's defined the following dykes as part of the post-Roman Silchester defences: two dykes called Grim's Bank (referred to as Grim's Bank 1 and Grim's Bank 2) close to Aldermaston, another Grim's Bank at Aldworth, the dykes on Crookham Common and a now-destroyed dyke on Greenham Common called Bury's Bank.

Grim's Bank 1 between Aldermaston and Padworth is built in the space between two Roman roads; the road from Silchester to Bath and the Roman road between Silchester and Dorchester on Thames. Grim's Bank 1 is a straight bank and ditch. Grim's Bank 2 is on the other side of the Silchester to Dorchester on Thames road and appears to connect to Grim's Bank 1. Grim's Bank 2 possibly relates to an Iron Age hilltop site at Mortimer Common. The dyke was possibly a prehistoric dyke reused and extended to form a post-Roman defence.

Grim's Bank 1 was excavated by O'Neil in 1943 (O'Neil, Grim's Bank Padworth Berkshire) at Padworth. O'Neil assumed Grim's Bank was placed to take advantage of the Roman roads as it runs between the road from Silchester to Spen and the one from Silchester to Dorchester. The north end of Grim's Bank runs into the earthworks around Raven Hill and cuts a ditch on Raven Hill that is part of a promontory fort of presumed Iron Age date. So Grim's Bank post-dates it but how much later is unknown. The section cut by O'Neil shows no dating evidence but does show the possibility of timber revetting. In a footnote O'Neil says, 'In the absence of archaeological proof they (that is the Silchester dykes) may be dated to this period tentatively by comparison with similar works elsewhere e.g. Wansdyke.' This is a not a very convincing argument.

A rescue excavation on Grim's Bank 1 in 1978 (Astill) in advance of a new oil pipeline did not produce much more evidence. Only two sherds were found in the bank, which were not diagnostic. The excavator suggested that the bank was revetted. The excavator suggested that Grim's Bank was constructed in late prehistoric times, not the Roman or post-Roman period as pollen evidence from beneath the bank showed when it was constructed that the surrounding land was open pasture, not under cereal cultivation. This is only tentative evidence of a prehistoric date. Comparison of the section drawing to the sections cut by O'Neil suggests that parts of the bank may have been built at different times as the ditches are different sizes. The most recent excavation in 2005 by Oxford Archaeology showed the construction of Grim's Bank was similar to Aves Ditch and the Oxfordshire Grim's Ditches and that the ditch had silted up slowly over a long period of time (Cockin). There are other earthworks that may be linked to Grim's Bank and it may be part of a more complex earthwork. There is no firm evidence of a post-Roman date for Grim's Bank 1.

Grim's Bank 2 has not been excavated and lies on a different alignment to Grim's Bank 1. O'Neill thought Grim's Bank 2 along with two other dykes covered a settlement at Mortimer West End, though there is no evidence that there was a settlement there in Roman times.

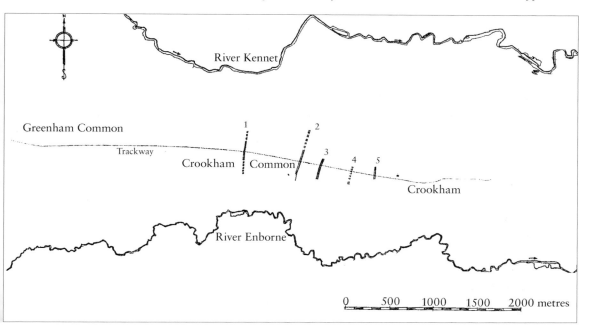

Map 9: The dykes on Greenham Common.

Bury's Bank on Greenham Common was flattened during the construction of Greenham Common airfield in the Second World War. O'Neil had excavated the dyke in advance of its destruction (O'Neil and Peake, A Linear Earthwork on Greenham Common Berkshire). Bury's Bank had a single phase and there is no evidence that the ditch was ever re-cut. Though the excavation found Roman sherds in the fill of the ditch it does not confirm a post-Roman date. Pottery from the ditch fill shows the latest vessel was fourth-century in date so the ditch could not have started to fill up before the fourth century. O'Neil suggests that the pottery was residual and the dyke is post-Roman. O'Neil suggested that the pottery fell into the ditch from the bank as it eroded as 'silting must have been rapid in the soil of Greenham Common'. Since O'Neil excavated in the 1940s evidence from experimental earthworks has challenged this view that a ditch would erode rapidly. It has been shown that ditches can stabilise and remain open for many years even in light sandy soils (Hillson).

Crookham Common is east of Greenham Common, closer to Silchester and has several earthworks. There are five possible dykes on Crookham Common: four certain and one earthwork, which is a bank between two ditches, more probably prehistoric than post-Roman. Only three of the dykes have ditches on the western side, facing away from Silchester. The dykes on Crookham Common have not been excavated.

About 17 km north, across the Thames, there is another Grim's Bank, the Aldworth to Streatley earthwork, which was included in the 'Chiltern Grim's Ditch' by O. G. S. Crawford (see Appendix). O'Neil instead included the Aldworth Grim's Ditch as an outlying defence of Silchester. O'Neil thought the Aldworth Grim's Ditch was intended to block the Ridgeway but was outflanked by the advancing Anglo-Saxons. The dykes closer to Silchester, Grim's Bank 1 and 2, are seen as a fallback to a second line of defence. Subsequent excavations by Ford of the Aldworth–Streatly Grim's Ditch (Ford, 'Linear Earthworks on the Berkshire Downs') produced Roman material from the ditch: 'On the basis of the Roman pottery the smaller of two ditches at Aldworth has a *terminus ante quem* in the later third century AD'.

Ford gives a date of 50 BC–AD 300 for the construction of the Aldworth–Streatley Grim's Ditch. Therefore the dyke cannot have anything to do with the post-Roman defence of Silchester.

There is also the problem with the Crookham Common and Greenham Common earthworks as part of Silchester's outer perimeter and western defences. They do not block a Roman road but across a trackway of unknown date. Also the five Crookham Common dykes are close together and do not make sense either as a defensive line or as a boundary. The Roman road from Silchester to Bath crossed over to the north bank of the River Kennet much closer to Silchester. There was no Anglo-Saxon threat from the west. O'Neil was forced to invent a trackway up from the south as a source of danger from Anglo-Saxons landing at Southampton Water.

Already by 1959 George Boon was questioning the idea of a Roman-British enclave around Silchester surviving for very long (Boon, 'The Latest Objects from Silchester, Hants'). Silchester was an Iron Age *oppidum* before it became the Roman town of Calleva Atrebatum. The *oppidum* was surrounded by an inner and outer earthwork (Boon, 'The Roman Town Calleva Atrebatum at Silchester Hampshire'). If Grim's Bank 1 and 2 are boundary markers, they may mark a territory relating to Iron Age Silchester instead of the post-Roman town.

Hampshire

Across the Surrey border in Hampshire, Grinsell suggested the dyke called the *Festean Dic* on Hartford Bridge Flats in north-east Hampshire was post-Roman in date. Others have suggested that it is a late medieval hundred boundary. Recent work by the North East Hampshire Historical and Archaeological Society (Whaley) has shown there are a series of dykes and terraces that overlie a possible Roman road. There is no firm evidence for dating and no excavation has yet taken place, but the positioning is suggestive. The dykes would control movement along the Roman road, possibly the line of Saxon advance from the Thames valley, but without further work this must remain in the uncertain category.

In Froxfield, close to Petersfield in Hampshire there are a whole series of earthworks. Coffin has suggested one of them, a dyke known as the Froxfield long entrenchments, was post-Roman and possibly formed the boundary of the kingdom of the Jutes that was known to exist in Hampshire. There is no archaeological evidence for the date of any the Froxfield dykes and the idea of the dyke being the boundary of an Anglo-Saxon kingdom must remain speculation.

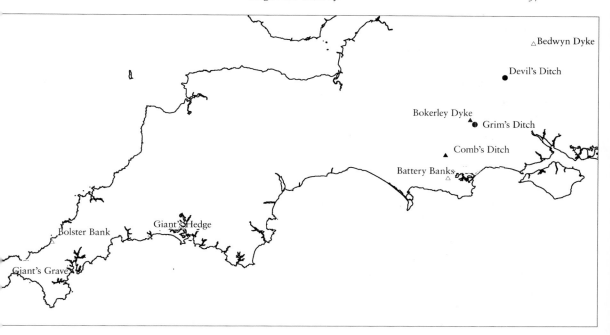

Map 10: Dykes in South West England.

The South West: Wiltshire, Avon, Cornwall and Dorset

Cornwall

> The devil one day having nothing to do,
> Built a great hedge from Lerrin to Looe
>   (Page)

O. G. S. Crawford suggested three dykes in Cornwall could be dated to the post-Roman period; the Giant's Hedge, Bolster Bank and the Giant's Grave. There has been no excavation on any of these Cornish dykes apart from a watching brief on a section cut through the Giant's Hedge. So it is impossible to confirm if any of these sites are prehistoric or post-Roman date.

The Giant's Hedge runs from Lerryn to Looe between two rivers, which with the earthwork define a block of territory with the sea on the south side. The linear earthwork runs east–west and survives in a variable state; some sections are well preserved while others have been removed. The bank is up to 4 m wide and in the better preserved sections the bank is up to 2.5 m high. There is a ditch on the north side though it cannot be seen along all sections of dyke, and may not exist. The course of the dyke is uncertain in several places. A watching brief took place when part of the dyke was cut though but found no dating evidence.

Bolster Bank is a linear earthwork of about 3 km long that cuts off St Agnes' beacon on the north Cornish coast. It consists of a bank and ditch, today with a height of about 3.5 m from top of the bank to the base of the ditch. It encloses an area of 5 sq. km. Parts of the monument have been destroyed but other sections survive well. Legend has it that a giant called Bolster constructed it, forcing St Agnes to help him carry the stones. There is no evidence for the Bolster Bank being of post-Roman date. It does not seem to relate to any known Roman road, unlike known post-Roman dykes. Johnson (Johnson) has pointed out that the Bolster Bank cuts off an area that was a valuable source of tin, but it is unlikely that tin was mined here before medieval times, only taken from surface sources. Another suggestion is that the Bolster Bank protected a Roman signal station on St Agnes' head.

The suggestion that the Giant's Grave was post-Roman comes from O. G. S. Crawford (O. G. Crawford, *The Work of Giants*). It has also been suggested as a Civil War entrenchment. Also there is a possibility that it once stretched from coast to coast, cutting off the Penwith peninsula, and making it more likely that it was prehistoric.

None of the Cornwall sites seem to be 'typical' dykes, if there is such a thing. The Bolster Bank is not really a linear earthwork at all and none of the dykes relate to the pattern of Roman roads or possible Romans roads. Dating these monuments is impossible without excavation and they are as likely to be prehistoric as Dark Age in date.

Dorset

Dorset has one dyke of post-Roman date and two dykes potentially of post-Roman date. The major dyke is Bokerley Dyke which has been investigated since the late nineteenth century.

Bokerley Dyke is a large earthwork about 6 km long that runs north-east across Cramborne Chase in Dorset from West Woodyates to Martin Wood. Bokerley Dyke blocks the Roman road from Salisbury (Old Sarum) to Dorchester, which is confusingly known as the Ackling Dyke. Bokerley Dyke has been badly damaged by ploughing and road widening for the A354 but survives well in the area away from the line of the road. The southern part of Bokerley Dyke still marks the county boundary between Dorset and Hampshire. The ditch is on the eastern side of the bank, so facing the direction of Old Sarum.

South of the Roman road Bokerley Dyke overlies and runs alongside part of a prehistoric dyke called Grim's Ditch, which is a Bronze Age or Iron Age boundary ditch (Piggot). Grim's Ditch runs for about 22 km across Cramborne Chase, and is a double-banked structure with a ditch between the banks. Grim's Ditch has sometimes been confused with Bokerley Dyke.

Bokerley Dyke consists of three sections; a section south of the Roman road and the modern road; a section known as the Rear Dyke and a section known as the Fore Dyke. The relationship between these parts of the dyke has been debated since the time of Pitt Rivers. Where the dyke crossed the Roman road the dyke consists of two parallel dykes known as the Rear Dyke and the Fore Dyke. The bank of the Rear Dyke has been almost completely destroyed.

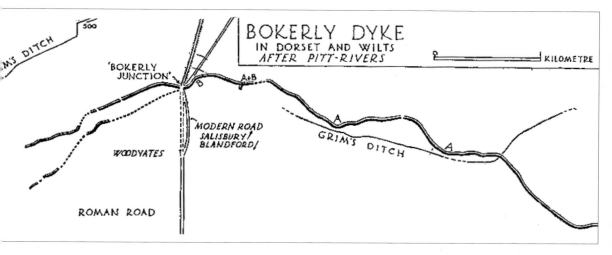

Map 11: Bokerly Dyke and the Grim's Ditch on Cramborne Chase after Pitt Rivers.

The archaeology of Bokerley Dyke is complex, and difficult to disentangle. A brief outline is something like this. By the fourth century a small Roman settlement existed to the east of the line of Bokerley Dyke. This has been described as a small settlement, without substantial structures unlike other known Roman roadside settlements, but has produced much pottery and many coins. Excavation conditions may explain this. Pitt Rivers' excavations of the 1890s may have simply missed the subtle traces of timber structures, and later excavations concentrated on the parts of the Dyke that were under threat of destruction by road building, not on the settlement area. In the late Roman period the Rear Dyke was dug across the Roman road for about 100 m, blocking it, but was apparently unfinished. The ditch was later filled in and the road re-laid across the dyke. After an unknown lapse of time the Fore Dyke was constructed. Again the purpose was to block the line of the road. This blocking is likely to be post-Roman. The RCHME in *The Archaeology of Bokerley Dyke* (H. C. Bowen) is equivocal about the function of the dyke at this period: 'It at least looks like a frontier – impossible to ignore but, equally, not truly defensive'. The final form of Bokerley Dyke was a single earthwork of post-Roman date. There is no evidence for how long Bokerley Dyke continued to act as a frontier but the Roman road between Salisbury and Dorchester went out of use completely. The modern A354 follows the line of an eighteenth-century turnpike road not the Roman road.

The next linear earthwork in Dorset is Comb's Ditch. Comb's Ditch is found on Charlton Down in the parish of Winterbourne Whitechurch, south of Blandford Forum. It was once at least 6.4 km long but only 4.4 km is now visible. It still forms the parish boundary between several Dorset parishes. It was once thought that it formed a second line of defence to Bokerley Dyke.

The dyke lies to the north of the Roman road from Badbury Rings to Dorchester. There is no evidence that it ever reached as far as the road line. There has been little fieldwork or excavation on the dyke, unlike Bokerley Dyke. The limited excavation seems to show a small dyke or field boundary being enlarged into a defensive earthwork. The bank of Comb's Ditch seals Iron Age pottery sherds, giving a *terminus post quem*. Excavation also found third- or fourth-century Roman pottery lying on the turf line behind the bank probably before its final reconstruction (P. J. Fowler, 'Interim Report on an Excavation in Combs Ditch Dorset, 1964'). Unfortunately there is no further evidence to pin down the date of the dyke more precisely. There is a strong suggestion that Comb's Ditch was originally an Iron Age boundary ditch but with late Roman or post-Roman refortification which would obviously have strong parallels with Bokerley Dyke.

Battery Banks is another candidate for a post-Roman dyke. There are four dykes to the east of Wareham in Dorset, on the ground between the River Piddle (or Trent) and the River Frome. The westernmost of these dykes, which runs north-west to south-east, is known as Battery Banks. The western dykes, referred to as the Worgret Dykes, run across the ridge of land separating the Frome and the Trent, possibly they once ran all the way between the rivers and cut off a section of land. One of these dykes passes around a round barrow, suggesting a post-Bronze Age date. It has been suggested by the RCHME that the Worgret dykes are Romano-British in date, because they parallel similar dykes on Cramborne Chase. Battery Banks which post-dates the Worgret Dykes would then be of post-Roman date. All these dykes have been badly damaged by erosion and by gravel extraction since the nineteenth century. The small-scale excavations that have taken place (Coe and Hawkes) have failed to find any dating evidence for the dykes. The Worgret Dykes are possibly related to animal management on the heath land. The dates of these dykes and the relationship between Battery Banks and the other dykes are at present unanswered questions. Christopher Taylor (Taylor, Dorset) links Bokerley Dyke with Comb's Ditch and Battery Banks as successive lines of post-Roman defence against Anglo-Saxon invaders pressing down from Salisbury.

The Wansdyke

The two sections of the Wansdyke form one of the most imposing monuments in Britain, similar in scale to Offa's Dyke or Hadrian's Wall. There are two earthworks, the East Wansdyke and the West Wansdyke, which cover the approaches to Wiltshire and (the old county of) Somerset respectively. The major survey of the Wansdyke was done by Cyril and Aileen Fox in 1958 (Fox & Fox). East Wansdyke runs east from the Savernake Forest along the chalk ridge overlooking the Kennet valley to Morgan's Hill north-west of Devizes. The west Wansdyke runs from a point south of Bath to Maes Knoll hillfort. Both the east and west Wansdyke are referred to as *Wodnesdic* (Woden's Dyke) in Anglo-Saxon charters, hence the assumption that they were a single monument. Both the east and west Wansdyke are earthworks with a single bank and a ditch on the north side.

Fox & Fox found no trace of the Wansdyke between the end of the East Wansdyke at Morgan's Hill and the beginning of the West Wansdyke at Horsecombe. Antiquaries such as Richard Colt Hoare had assumed that the dyke continued along the line of the Roman road between *Verucio* (Sandy Lane) and Bath making a single monument.

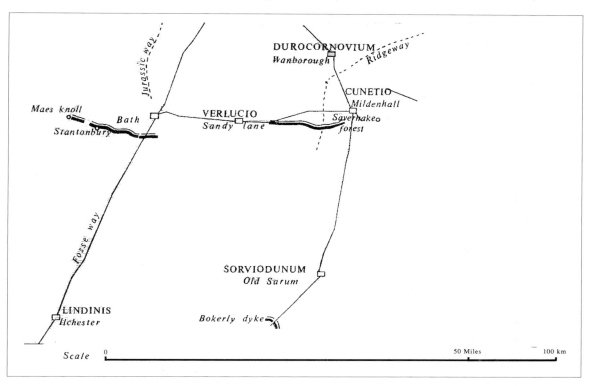

Map 12: The West and East Wansdyke.

It is unfortunate that the agger of the Roman road was mistaken for the bank of the dyke here. Fox & Fox argued that the dyke does not exist here as the land was sparsely populated in Roman times and 'hostile north to south movement in such an area would be most unlikely'. It is unfortunate there has been no serious ground investigation of the section between the west and east Wansdyke since the Fox's investigations of the 1950s.

The Foxs' conclusions that there were two separate dykes of different dates has not been really challenged since, though there have been objections to the idea that the West Wansdyke stops at Maes Knoll and does not continue on to the Bristol Channel (Gardiner).

The West Wansdyke

The west Wansdyke crosses Bath and north-east Somerset from Maes Knoll in the west to Horsecombe in the east and is 14 km long. The dyke faces north or north-east. Unlike the East Wansdyke, the position of the West Wansdyke is not commanding, and is overlooked by higher ground. The west Wansdyke does have some large gaps. There are three gaps in the dyke: at Publow Hill 1.6 km wide; east of English Comb 1.2 km wide and at Pennsylvania Farm 0.4 km wide. No traces of the dyke have been found

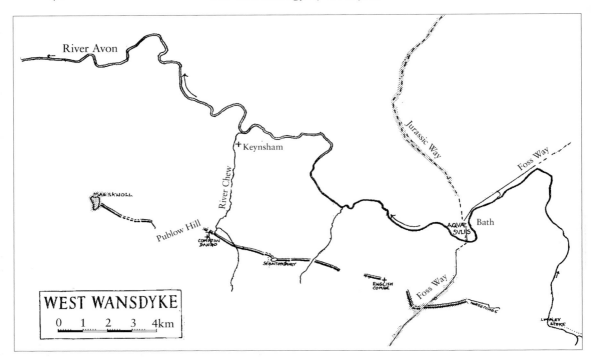

Map 13: The West Wansdyke.

in these gaps either using air photographs or by field work. There is no sign of any revetment or a palisade on the West Wansdyke.

The course of the Wansdyke from west to east is from Maes Knoll hillfort where Fox & Fox have the monument stop before the earthworks of the hillfort. Then there is the large gap on Publow Hill which Fox & Fox claim is due to thick woodland when the dyke was constructed. Fox & Fox saw no evidence of the Wansdyke meeting the defences of Stantonbury hillfort, but Gardiner shows that the Wansdyke runs right up to the defences of Stantonbury. Stantonbury Camp does not seem to have any traces of post-Roman occupation, but has not been excavated.

Further on the dyke is crossed by one of the supposed branches of the 'Jurassic Way' recorded as a '*herepath*' in a Bath Abbey Charter of AD 963. The Wansdyke ends suddenly at Horsecombe Valley. Like the East Wansdyke the West Wansdyke uses large hills as viewpoints. From Stantonbury Camp the whole of the West Wansdyke can be seen on a clear day. The west Wansdyke bank and ditch is much smaller than the East Wansdyke sections built on chalk but is comparable in size to the East Wansdyke in its forest sections.

Gardner in The Wansdyke Diktat (Gardiner), shows that antiquarian opinion extended the West Wansdyke beyond Maes Knoll across Aston Vale. Gardner shows that there are 'extant, maybe unfinished, and albeit even irrelevant linear earthworks between Dundry and the Avon Gorge' and that contrary to Fox & Fox the Wansdyke does run into the defences of Maes Knoll hillfort as it does at Stantonbury Camp.

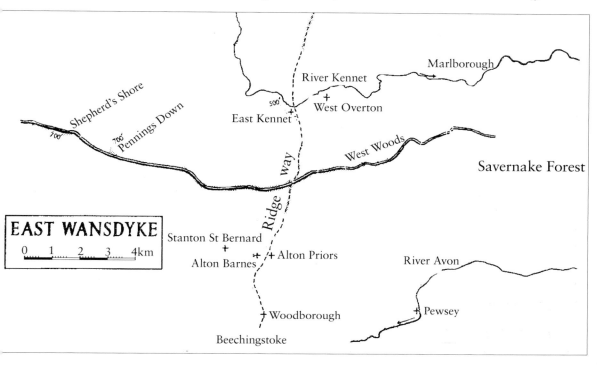

Map 14: The East Wansdyke.

The purpose of the West Wansdyke seems to be to control movement down the Fossway, the Roman road from Bath, protecting Somerset from incursions down the Avon valley and the Cotswolds. Fox & Fox suggest the dyke builders had lost control of the Avon crossings but an alternative explanation could be that the dyke forms a defensive line behind the boundary of the Avon, being built on the first defensible high ground behind the Avon. The land between the Wansdyke and the Avon would then form a frontier zone.

The East Wansdyke

The east Wansdyke is a massive monument, with a bigger bank and ditch than Offa's Dyke, Wat's Dyke or Bokerley Dyke. The only dyke with a bigger bank is the Devil's Dyke in Cambridgeshire. The east Wansdyke from Morgan's Hill to Savernake Forest is 21 km long. The width of bank and ditch is up to 28 m wide in some places. The angle of the bank and ditch is about 30 degrees making it very difficult to climb. The east Wansdyke is much smaller in size at the eastern end, where the chalk soil changes to clay. Fox & Fox assume that the Wansdyke was a military barrier on the chalk and a territorial barrier on the heavier soils. The dyke has sections that are straight, some that are sinuous and some that are irregular suggesting that different work gangs built different sections. This is very similar to the construction of Offa's Dyke. Like the West Wansdyke there is no sign of any revetment along the East Wansdyke and the top is rounded suggesting that there was no walkway or palisade present. A counter-scarp bank exists for some parts of the East Wansdyke to reinforce it. It is not known if this counter-scarp existed all along the dyke.

The dyke is in a commanding position over the land to the north-east and the dyke is normally constructed on the forward slope of hills apart from a section on the reverse slope of Morgan's Hill which would otherwise lead to a large salient. Pitt Rivers sectioned Wansdyke here and found Romano-British coarse pottery under the bank confirming a Roman or post-Roman date for the earthwork. A second Pitt Rivers section found part of the Wansdyke built over a Romano-British enclosure.

The section from Tan Hill to Red Shore gives a superb view over the Kennet valley; invaders are visible as far as the Marlborough Downs. From the top of Tan Hill the whole of the dyke could also be seen. At Red Shore a drove road crosses the dyke and it is mentioned by a ninth-century charter as 'thaet Riad Geat', the Red Gate. The Wansdyke enters Savernake Forest and simply stops. Antiquarians such as Richard Colt Hoare believed the Wansdyke once extended east to cover central Wiltshire. Also O. G. S. Crawford thought the Wansdyke incorporated the Bedwyn Dykes and a section of earthwork at Inkpen in Berkshire that was referred to as 'Wans Dyke' in an enclosure award map of AD 1733.

Fox & Fox note that two Roman roads cross Savernake Forest, the one to Old Sarum and the one to Winchester. There is no trace of the dyke around them so it was assumed that they were overgrown and out of use by the time that the dyke was built. This has been challenged by Peter Fowler (P. Fowler) who suggests the East Wansdyke was built on Roman military model, by someone who had knowledge of Roman frontier defences such as Hadrian's Wall. The eastern end of the Wansdyke, in the West Woods of Overton and Fyfield parishes, is unfinished with only 4.5 km of dyke in the woods. In these woods the Wansdyke is made of a series of dumps, 0.5–0.75 m high, with a ditch that is discontinuous either filled in or never dug. Fowler estimated the building of the West Woods section of Wansdyke took twenty to thirty days by 1,000 men, or two to three thousand man-days.

There are up to ten gates in this part of the Wansdyke, with good documentary evidence for four gates in the tenth century. One of the possible gates *Eadgardes* has evidence of outworks. Fowler sees the gates controlling existing routes and the gates as intended to be manned even if in practise they were not as Wansdyke is unfinished. The aim was to control movement not prevent it. The tracks were not built later; Wansdyke was built to control traffic on existing routes from the north to south.

Fowler shows that the gates were 1.5 or 0.5 Roman miles apart and compares them to the fortlets on Hadrian's Wall linking Wansdyke with Roman military design. The use of Roman measurements is not conclusive for dating the Wansdyke. There are a number of Viking ring forts in Denmark and southern Sweden called Trelleborg that are laid out using Roman measurements.

Fowler prefers a late fifth-century date for Wansdyke. In the AD 490s the threat was from Anglo-Saxons of the Thames Valley that disappeared after the Battle of Badon. The major question is why is the East Wansdyke only unfinished on the eastern end? If it was built in sections by local labour it should be unfinished elsewhere but the East

Wansdyke appears to be complete on the chalk downlands. An explanation could be that the east end of Wansdyke was an unfinished extension of the monument, possibly designed to control the Roman roads through the Savernake Forest. Then the question of date becomes more complex. The Wansdyke may have been unfinished because the potential threat disappeared or it may have been stopped because the builders of Wansdyke were successfully outflanked.

Dating of the Wansdyke

The date of both the west and east Wansdyke has been the subject of much debate. The evidence from excavation gives a *terminus post quem* of the mid-third century AD for both dykes. The options for dating of both the west and east Wansdyke include:

A boundary between sub-Roman groups in the fifth century.
Built by the post-Roman British against a Saxon threat in the late fifth century.
A boundary between the Anglo-Saxon kingdoms in the sixth or seventh century.

For both monuments Fox & Fox preferred the third option, specifically the East Wansdyke being the work of Ceawlin ruler of the Gewissæ against a threat from the Saxons of the Thames valley, while they see the West Wansdyke as the work of Cynegils of Wessex, against Penda of Mercia after AD 628.

Others have preferred earlier dates. Erskine claims that the West Wansdyke could be as early as the late Roman period, though his evidence was circumstantial. Gardiner sees the West Wansdyke as the boundary of a political entity based on either Gatcombe, which was a late Roman defended establishment, or on the hillfort of Cadbury Congresbury, built by the British against a Saxons threat in the late fifth century after the Anglo-Saxons had captured the Cotswolds. Fowler sees the East Wansdyke as an unfinished monument against an Anglo-Saxon threat from the Thames valley that was rendered obsolete by the British victory at Badon. Green suggests a date between AD 450 to AD 500 or AD 550 to AD 600. Green's suggestion is that both west and east Wansdyke were built by the Anglo-Saxon Cerdicings against Ceaswlin who was a prince of the Thames Valley Saxons, but also a possible suggestion that Wansdyke was partly earlier between Morgan's Hill and Shaw House.

One further possibility is that the Roman road formed part of the boundary and linked the two dykes into a single monument. A palisade may have been enough to mark the line of the boundary in this section, though there is no archaeological evidence for this. In this scenario the Wansdyke would only have been needed to be built where there was no existing boundary marker such as the Roman road.

The Bedwyn Dyke

Until the work of the Foxes it was assumed the fragments of dykes beyond Savernake Forest were part of the Wansdyke. These include two small fragments of dyke in Little Bedwyn parish. The major earthwork once believed to part of Wansdyke is the Bedwyn Dyke, a single bank and ditch facing north, about 2.4 km long. The Bedwyn Dyke starts

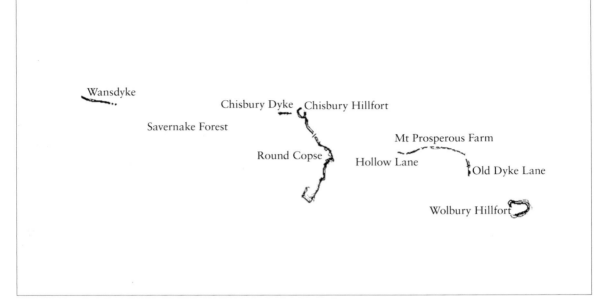

Wansdyke

Chisbury Dyke Chisbury Hillfort

Savernake Forest

Mt Prosperous Farm

Round Copse

Hollow Lane

Old Dyke Lane

Wolbury Hillfort

Map 15: The Bedwyn Dyke.

below Chisbury Hillfort and may once have extended up to it. It is comparable in size to the East Wansdyke; together the width of bank and ditch is 17.8 m. Fox & Fox don't consider it to be part of the Wansdyke but link it to Cissa a seventh- or eighth-century sub-king of Wessex. Chisbury Hillfort may be derived from his name. Fox & Fox suggest the dyke may mark the boundary of the original Anglo-Saxon Bedwyn estate.

Hosttetter & Howe in their 1986 survey question the idea of a Bedwyn Dyke 'system' and point out how fragmented the dyke is, with plenty of gaps between parts of the dyke. Many of the dykes are heavily eroded. Were these gaps really filled by forest? Many sections of dyke run below a ridge line like the Wansdyke. The dyke is not really defensive even with a palisade on top. Hosttetter and Howe suggest the Bedwyn dyke was a Roman estate boundary to mark the original extent of the estate based on the Bedwyn Roman villa. However until excavation can provide any evidence then the date and purpose of the Bedwyn dyke must remain unknown.

The Eastern Counties: Cambridgeshire, Norfolk and Suffolk

The Cambridgeshire Dykes
The four dykes in Cambridgeshire are certainly post-Roman in date and while three of them only survive in a poor state, the construction method of the Devil's Dyke means it survives as a spectacular monument, cutting a straight line through the flat

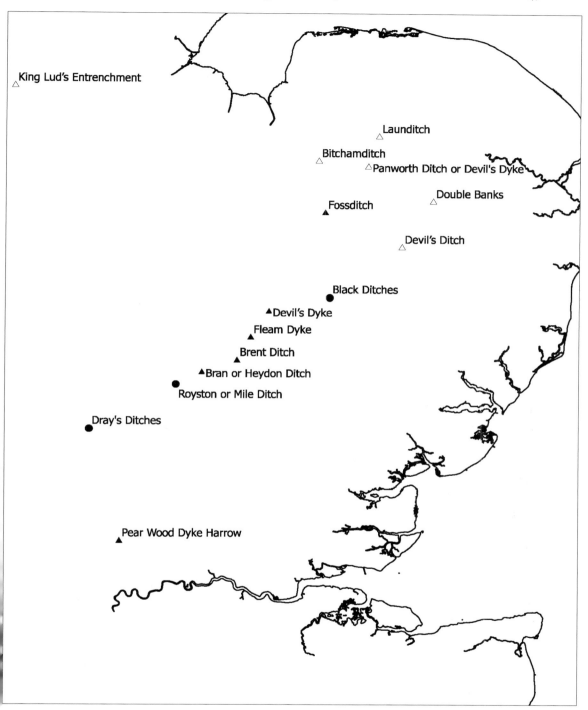

King Lud's Entrenchment

Launditch

Bitchamditch

Panworth Ditch or Devil's Dyke

Double Banks

Fossditch

Devil's Ditch

Black Ditches

Devil's Dyke

Fleam Dyke

Brent Ditch

Bran or Heydon Ditch

Royston or Mile Ditch

Dray's Ditches

Pear Wood Dyke Harrow

Map 16: Dykes in Eastern England.

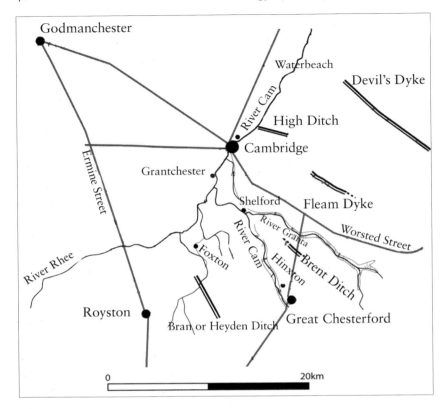

Map 17: The Cambridge Dykes.

Cambridgeshire landscape. 'It is a strange and brooding eminence, particularly in thick fog and out of season' (Bryson).

The four dykes are from south-west to north-east: The Bran or Heydon Ditch; the Brent Ditch; the Fleam Dyke and the Devil's Dyke. The Black Ditches in Suffolk and the Royston Ditch (or Mile Ditches) in Hertfordshire were once regarded as related to the Cambridgeshire dyke system but excavations have shown both these dykes are more likely Iron Age in date.

The Bran or Heydon Ditch has been almost totally flattened and can only be seen as an old field boundary. It runs for 5 km from Heydon, north-west to Black Peak. Heydon is on the edge of a clay plateau and the dyke runs across the chalk to the wetlands at Black Peak. Fox's excavations established a *terminus post quem* of the third century AD for the construction of the dyke. Modern excavations (Malim, New evidence on the Cambridgeshire Dykes and Warstead Street Roman Road) have shown a single phase of construction and the northern end of the dyke was filled with water. The wetlands at the northern end of the Bran Ditch may have made any further extension of the dyke unnecessary.

The northern part of the Brent Ditch is a visible earthwork while the southern part of the dyke is seen as a shallow depression in the ground. The Brent Ditch is cut through by the modern A11 road. There is no evidence of a massive bank, just slight ridges on either side of the ditch. Either the ditch had a very wide berm or no bank as the ditch section shows the ditch being infilled symmetrically. Excavation recovered five Roman coins the latest a *sestertius* of Commodus (AD 180–192).

The Fleam Dyke is the most complicated of all the Cambridgeshire Dykes. There are three parts to the dyke. The main section of the dyke, also called the Balsham Ditch runs northwards from Oxcroft Farm near Balsham to Shardelow's Well on Ashwell Street, a Roman Road. This is the Fleam Dyke proper. At the southern end of the dyke it only survives as a hedge bank. Also it has been cut through by the A11. Then there is the 'northern extension' from Shardelow's Well to Great Wilbraham Fen. Then there is the High Ditch at Fen Ditton. The relationship between the High Ditch and the Fleam Ditch is uncertain. The RCHME (Royal Commission on Historical Monuments (England) has argued that it is separate to the Fleam Ditch and possibly prehistoric. Before the drainage of the Fens, High Ditch would have blocked the space between two rivers creating a defensible area of land. The village of Fen Ditton uses the dyke as its main street, possibly showing that it was abandoned at an early date. There have been no archaeological excavations on the High Ditch. Anglo-Saxon burials were found in the fill of High Ditch in 1957 but not excavated archaeologically; they were disturbed by road building (Lethbridge, *The Riddle of the Dykes*). All the excavations have taken place on the Fleam Dyke proper.

The most recent excavations took place in 1991 and 1992 when the A11 was widened. The buried soil under the bank of the Fleam Ditch had 'pulverised' Roman pottery of the first and second century AD in it. The excavation showed a guide bank of turf was used to construct the centre of the bank. There is a possible fourth-century coin from the bank. A radiocarbon date of 330–510 cal. AD at 95 per cent confidence level was obtained from the ditch. The date of the dyke is most likely the early Saxon period. The bank was raised in a number of stages most likely by adding material from the cleaning of the ditches. The first stage of the ditch was a V-shaped ditch that was widened to a wide flat-bottomed ditch. The radiocarbon dates can accommodate a construction within the sixth century AD and a final use between AD 590 and 700 (Malim, 'New evidence on the Cambridgeshire Dykes and Warstead Street Roman Road'). The Fleam Dyke is different from the others, more winding and seems to show a major re-cut of the ditch.

The Devil's Dyke is the most impressive and best preserved of all the Cambridgeshire Dykes and of the Dark Age dykes possibly only Wansdyke and Offa's Dyke are more spectacular. The dyke is 11 km long and the central section is very straight and impressive in the flat landscape of the fens. The ends of the dyke curve away. Cyril Fox (C. Fox, *The Archaeology of the Cambridge Region*) believed that this showed the builders did not know how to lay out a long straight line beyond the line of sight as the Romans would have done. The angle of the bank ensures that the bank is very stable and so very little fill is present in the ditch. Excavation shows there is a single phase with no re-cutting of the ditch. There is a causeway called the 'Cambridgeshire Gap' on Newmarket racecourse where Ashwell Street crosses the dyke. The causeway seems to be an original part of the dyke. The Devil's Dyke is engineered in a single phase and is so well constructed that it needed no rebuilding or re-cutting.

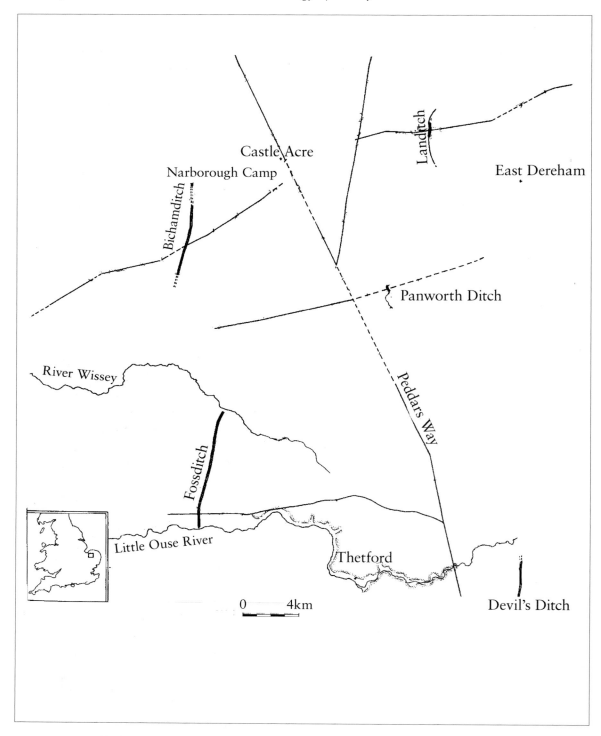

Map 18: Dykes in Norfolk.

The name Devil's Dyke is post-medieval; in medieval documents both the Devil's Dyke and the Fleam Ditch are referred to as simply 'the dic' or the great ditch. Fleam derives from the old English for flight but why it should be applied to the dyke is unknown. Devil's Dyke was also known as St Edmund's Dyke as it marked the limit of the diocese of Bury St Edmunds, or alternatively as the Reach Dyke. The Bran and Brent Ditches each have an early form in *Brang* or *Brank*, but it is not known what the name means.

The supposed line of the 'Icknield Way' is cut at right-angles by the dykes but the dykes also block a number of Roman roads that run parallel to or at obtuse angles to the dykes.

Tim Malim (Malim, 'New evidence on the Cambridgeshire Dykes and Warstead Street Roman Road') suggests a pattern from west to east of bigger ditches showing improvement in the construction techniques so the Devil's Ditch would be the latest of the series but there is no definite dating evidence for this sequence.

Norfolk

There are a number of dykes in Norfolk that have been considered of likely post-Roman date. In addition to the dykes marked on the OS Dark Age maps, a number are listed in the Gazetteer.

The Fossditch is the only one of the Norfolk dykes which is firmly dated to the post-Roman period because Roman pot sherds were found under the dyke in a section cut by R. Rainbird Clarke. The line of the dyke runs between the River Wissey and the River Ouse, cutting off the land between the two rivers. It blocks the line of a possible Roman road. The Fossditch was once thought to be a Roman road, and was first described as a dyke by Charles Babington. Even in Babington's time, 1854, it was described as being much destroyed by cultivation. The ditch is on the east side so the dyke faces east, not as the Ordnance Survey Dark Age maps have it, facing west.

Bichamditch or Devil's Dyke is assumed to be post-Roman but only medieval and post-medieval finds have been found in the ditch fills. It is built in a straight line from Beachamwell to Narborough, 8 km long. At one end of the Bichamditch is the Iron Age hillfort of Narborough Camp. The relationship between the two monuments is unknown. This dyke also faces east, not west as shown on the OS map.

The Launditch has been traced for over 6 km but now less than 1 km survives as an upstanding earthwork. It is very straight in the central section but curves eastwards at each end. An unpublished 1992 excavation by the Norfolk Archaeology Unit suggests it is cut by a Roman road and could be Iron Age in date.

The extant lengths of the Bichamditch and the Fossditch are much longer than the known lengths of the Launditch and the Panworth Ditch. Peter Wade-Martins (Wade-Martins) points out that the Ordnance Survey Dark Age maps show the Bichamditch and Fossditch facing the wrong way, west instead of east. Wade-Martins suggest there are two pairs of opposing dykes, built facing each other, leading to an idea of some kind of buffer zone or demilitarised zone between the dykes. Unfortunately this idea breaks down if the dykes are not all of the same date.

Suffolk

The Black Ditches is in the parish of Cavenham in Suffolk between the River Lark and Cavenham Brook. Despite the name there is only one ditch. About 1 km of ditch survives on a north–south alignment. A now detached length of the ditch forms the parish boundary between Cavenham and Lackford. It had been assumed that the Black Ditches is post-Roman in date on analogy with the Cambridgeshire Dykes, blocking the Icknield Way between the Lark valley and the higher ground. The Suffolk Archaeological Unit carried out a cleaning and recording exercise in 1992 where the ditch had been cut away for gravel extraction. This showed the dyke had a ditch on each side of the bank – it was bivallate. The ditch on the west side was bigger than the one on the east side. Also late Iron Age pottery sherds were found in the eastern ditch. The pottery does not prove the monument was of Iron Age date but it strongly suggests that it could be prehistoric. This would be a similar case to the Miles Ditches in Hertfordshire.

The Midlands

Derbyshire

Derbyshire has one certain post-Roman dyke and two possible post-Roman monuments. The Grey Ditch, near Bradwell in the Peak District is a certain post-Roman earthwork. The dyke is constructed at right angles to the Roman road called the Batham Gate, which runs between the Roman fort at Brough in Derbyshire (the Roman name was *Navio*) and the Roman settlement at Buxton (*Aquae Arnemetiae*).

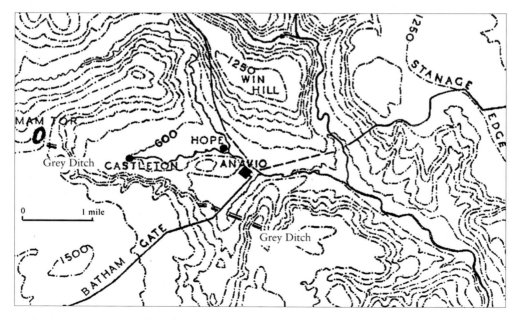

Map 19: Dykes in Derbyshire.

When first recorded the length of the Grey Ditch earthwork was about 1.7 km long; it now has substantial gaps, caused by ploughing and by development along the road line. The monument runs across the contours, crossing the Batham Gate and a river called the Bradwell brook. Any movement along the road would be controlled and it would be difficult to go around the Grey Ditch. Presumably the threat was from the north-east as the ditch is on this side. The bank seems to have a single phase while the ditch showed evidence of up to five re-cuts. Importantly the bank lay over a plough soil, which contained sherds of Roman-British pottery. B. H. O'Neil (O'Neil, *Grey Ditch, Bradwell, Derbyshire*) following the Victoria county history suggests the Grey Ditch once carried as far as the slopes of Mam Tor. However there is no firm evidence for this, further survey or aerial photography evidence is needed to prove this point.

Two other earthworks have been suggested to be post-Roman earthwork; the Calver Cross Ridge Dyke and the Longstone Edge Cross Ridge Dyke, both because they are similar in form to the Grey Ditch. Neither has been excavated.

This area marks the boundary between the *Pecsaetna* (people of the Peak District) and the kingdom of Mercia and the dykes here could be boundary markers between these groups, however further evidence is needed.

Oxfordshire

There are three dykes in Oxfordshire: the Aves Ditch, the North Oxfordshire Grim's Ditch and the South Oxfordshire Grim's Ditch, which are now all known to be Iron Age in date but were once considered as post-Roman. Details of these earthworks are given in the gazetteer. The Aves Ditch is an interesting case, definitely constructed in the Iron Age it may have continued to be used as a boundary marker into Anglo-Saxon period as it was used for an Anglo-Saxon burial. The burial was of a woman and a short time after burial her skull had been removed cleanly from her skeleton (Sauer).

Yorkshire

The Scot's Dyke

The Scot's Dyke, also spelt Scots Dyke or Scots Dike, is a linear earthwork about 14 km long running from the Swale to the Tees. It was mentioned by Camden in the 1580s and the name 'Scots Dike' first mentioned in a letter of 1723 (Smith). The dyke runs from south to north, from Eastby on the Swale to a point between the village of Aldbrough St John and the earthworks of the Iron Age *oppidum* of Stanwick. Clarkson in his History of Richmond (Clarkson) claims the dyke had once extended to the Scottish lowlands and further into Yorkshire.

This mound enters from Scotland at a place called WHEELFEEL, between the Rivers North Tyne and Read, and cutting the Roman Road at Busy.Gap, soon after crosses South Tyne, and falls in with the River Allen; the banks of which being very steep, answer the end for which such a trench was made. Soon after it appears again at a place called Sporn Gate

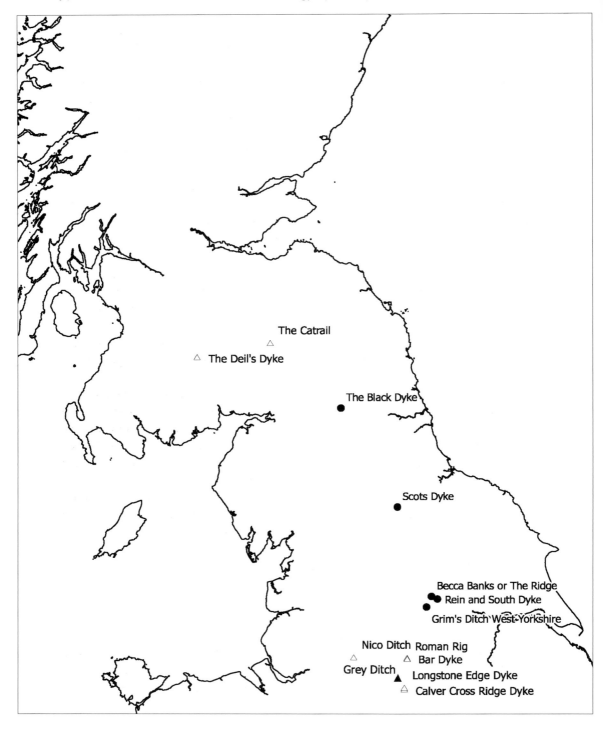

Map 20: Northern England and Southern Scotland.

Cross, where the mound is very conspicuous, and is called Scot's-Nick. There it enters the County of Durham, and points towards the head of the River Tees, which is the course of it to Winstone. Crossing the Tees here, this stupendous work stretches by Stanwick over the Watling Street on Gatherly-Moor, and coming this way through Whitefield Pasture, where it appears in an almost perfect state, passes the Swale at Hind Wath, in Low Bank Bouse Ing. Going up St. Martin's Pasture, it extends by Sandbeck, over Hudswell-Moor, and probably much further into Yorkshire, if not quite through it.

(Clarkson, 1814)

The dyke occupies high ground with good views to the east, and it is not straight but curves and has angular changes in the northern section. A link with the earthworks of Stanwick would be logical but there is no evidence of one, despite the Ordnance Survey maps showing a link to Stanwick. Smith (Smith) quotes an unpublished RCHME survey of 1964 that dismisses such a link or any evidence of a northward extension of the dyke to the Tees. Extensive labour was needed to build the Scot's Dyke, and it varies in size and form throughout its length, showing that each section was built by a separate labour gang. Parts of the dyke are possibly a double dyke as shown by the Ordnance Survey maps at the northern end of the dyke.

Smith supported the claim of a post-Roman date for the dyke linking it with two other Swaledale dykes at Reeth and Fremington. Both the Reeth and Fremington dykes cross the Swale valley 14 km upstream from Richmond. The Reeth dyke is 2 km long and the Fremington dyke 1 km long. Both are single bank dykes, with a ditch on the eastern side with a counterscarp. Smith claimed the purpose of the Scot's Dyke was to protect the eastern boundary of the British kingdom of Rheged from Saxon incursions.

Excavations in advance of the A66 improvements between Carkin Moor and Scotch Corner gave an opportunity for the dyke to be investigated. Excavation work was carried out by Oxford Archaeology North. No artefacts were recovered from the excavation and the relationship between the Scot's Dyke and the Roman road was not established by the excavations. Fortunately samples of the ditch fills were taken for archaeomagnetic dating and optically stimulated luminescence (OSL) dating.

The OSL evidence suggests that the lower part of the dike was probably silting up during the period between the first century BC and the first century AD. The uppermost date would suggest that it was still silting at the end of the Romano-British period or shortly thereafter.

(Oxford Archaeology North)

The archaeomagnetic dating also suggests that the fill of the Scot's Dyke was formed rapidly during the first century AD (Karloukovski and Hounslow). It seems that the Scot's Dyke was built in the late Iron Age and went out of use in the Roman period.

The Aberford Dykes

The Aberford dykes are just outside the modern town of Aberford positioned where the Roman road north from Castleford to Tadcaster crosses the stream called the

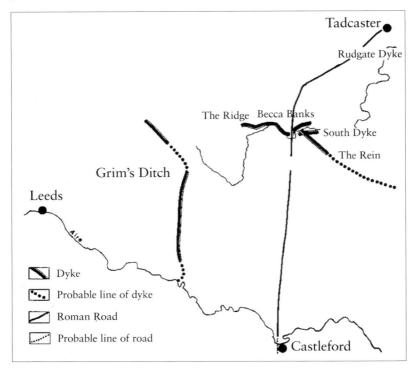

Map 21: Dykes in West Yorkshire after Wilmott.

Cock Beck. Aberford is about 13 km north of Castleford. The dykes lie on top of the scarp of Magnesian limestone that runs at a right angle to the road. The Roman road became the Great North Road which was the main route to the north up to the twentieth century. The modern A1(M) has replaced this road and runs on a line to the east of the modern Aberford village. The Aberford Dykes were known about by antiquarians since the time of John Leland: 'Thet ly by est of Aberford 2. or 3. long ditches as campes of men of warre' (John Leland *The Itinerary* AD 1535).

There were three main suggestions about the date and functions of the Aberford dykes:

> Iron Age in date, the frontier defences of the Brigantes, and may be a reaction against Roman expansion in the late first century AD.
> The dykes are post-Roman marking the boundary of the British kingdom of Elmet, against Anglo-Saxon expansion from the kingdom of Deira.
> The dykes are Anglo-Saxon work; the defences of the kingdom of Deira against Mercian expansion from the Midlands.

The dykes are substantial works and the number of dykes suggests use over a long period of time. There are four dykes, the most westerly of which is called The Ridge. This is separated by a small wooded area from the next part of the main dyke known as Becca Banks. The dyke runs along the north bank of the Cock Beck, using the scarp to increase the height of the bank.

East of the A1 and south of the Cock Beck are the two other dykes, The Rein and the South Dyke. The Rein is a straight dyke, cutting across the South Dyke and therefore later in date. The South Dyke ends 'in air' and this may be the reason it was replaced by the Rein. All of the dykes have ditches on the south side suggesting a threat coming from the direction of Castleford. As the dykes end where the heavier soils begin it has been suggested that they had thick woodland forming a natural barrier at their ends (Alcock).

The dykes had been linked to the post-Roman British kingdom of Elmet though Alcock pointed out that a number of Elmet names such as Barwick in Elmet and Sherburn in Elmet lie 'outside' of the dyke to the south. Attempts to link the dykes to the *regio* of Loidis described by Bede is unlikely as Leeds, Ledston, and Ledsham all names deriving from Loidis lie to the south of the dyke.

The date of the dykes had always been problematic. O. G. S. Crawford included them in the original Ordnance Survey Dark Age map but Alcock argued that the signs of revetment along Becca Banks (following Crawford's description) showed parallels with the Iron Age defences at Stanwick, the stone-revetted dyke on Minchinhampton Common and also the defences at Lexeden, Colchester. This stone revetment that Crawford saw on Becca Banks to the west side of Aberford has never been seen since but is likely to have been an outcrop of limestone mistaken for a revetment. Alcock also claimed there was an original entrance gap in Becca Banks to the west of the Roman road indicating that the dyke predated the road. The track leading to the ford and gap are unlikely to have been created after the Roman road was built.

Fortunately the construction of the new A1 M1 link road enabled excavations to take place on both the Aberford Dykes and the West Yorkshire Grim's Ditch (Roberts I & Berg).

The excavation shows that the ditch of the South Dyke had been re-cut several times. The fills of the ditch were water laid showing that the Cock Beck was once flowing along the ditch, which would reinforce the defences of the earthwork. The dating evidence shows a prehistoric date for the construction of the ditch with a Roman redefinition and filling in around the third century AD. The final fill of the ditch had medieval pottery in. There is no evidence of Dark Age activity but there is no dating evidence at all from beneath the bank.

The excavation found that Becca Banks overlay an enclosure ditch which was filled by bank construction material. This shows that the enclosure ditch was open at the time of Becca Bank's construction. One sherd of Iron Age or early Roman pottery gives a *terminus post quem* for the date of the enclosure. The excavator suggests that Becca Banks was built shortly after the enclosure. The filling of the ditch of Becca Banks has Roman pottery of the second century AD, but calibrated radiocarbon dates from animal bone in the ditch fill give dates of AD 559–671, and so the pottery is residual. The top fills of Becca Banks contain thirteenth-century pottery with some possible Saxon sherds. The date of construction suggested by the excavator is between the Iron Age to the seventh century AD, but more likely Becca Banks is Iron Age, like the South Dyke.

If the Aberford Dykes were ever used in the post-Roman period they went out of use rapidly. It is much more likely they are Iron Age in date.

The West Yorkshire Grim's Ditch

The West Yorkshire Grim's Ditch does not appear on either of the Ordnance Survey Dark Age maps as this dyke was only recognised in the 1970s through the work of Margaret Faull on the place names of West Yorkshire. It had escaped the attention of Yorkshire antiquarians of the eighteenth and nineteenth centuries mainly because of the poor state of preservation, the monument being ploughed away and built over in many places. Also one part of the monument had been known as the 'Roman Rig' and was interpreted as being part of a Roman road. This should not be confused with the Roman Ridge in South Yorkshire or the misidentified section of Roman road in West Yorkshire that appears on the OS Dark Age map as a dyke.

The West Yorkshire Grim's Ditch is situated between Leeds and Castleford and runs north south. The ditch is on the eastern side. The ditch runs from Whinmoor in the north to Swillington Bridge on the banks of the River Aire in the south, total length is about 10 km. The ditch is on the eastern side of the bank. The name 'Grim's Ditch' to refer to the whole monument is also a recent coinage; late medieval documents only refer to the northern section as Grim's Ditch. The Grim's Ditch needed substantial effort to build as the ditch was cut into the shale bedrock in parts.

The line of the ditch follows the edge of the Magnesian limestone, and like the Aberford Dykes uses the existing scarp to raise the height of the ditch. Where there is no existing scarp the ditch is deeper as it seems the high bank was the most important feature of this monument.

There were three main suggestions for a date for the Grim's Ditch; prehistoric; post-Roman, being a boundary for the kingdom of Elmet or for a political centre in based on Leeds, the *regio* of Loidis; or being a boundary between the Saxon kingdoms of Northumbria and Mercia.

Excavations prior to the upgrading of the A1(M) excavated two sections of the Grim's Ditch (Roberts I & Berg). The northern section only recovered artefacts from the upper fill of the ditch, mainly eighteenth-century pottery, glass and clay pipe fragments, as well as animal bone. Nothing was found under the bank. This was interpreted as deliberate infilling of the ditch in the eighteenth century. On the southern section, a radiocarbon date of AD 86–335 was obtained from charcoal in the primary fill of the ditch. Other dates of 777–396 BC and 790–400 BC were obtained from other fills. This suggests that Grim's Ditch was built in the first millennium BC and is Iron Age, with a possible redefinition in the late Roman period. There is no evidence for any reuse in the post-Roman period. The Grim's Ditch has been so degraded by industrial activity and agriculture that it is not possible to see if it is a single entity. The north end of the dyke is close to the end of the Aberford dykes near to the west end of the Ridge. The relationship between the Grim's Ditch and the Aberford dykes is intriguing and as yet unknown.

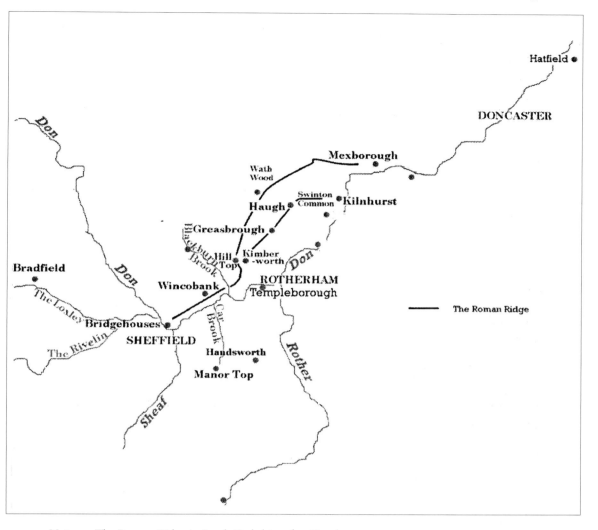

Map 22: The Roman Ridge in South Yorkshire after Cronk.

The Roman Ridge

The words most often applied to South Yorkshire's Roman Ridge (also called the Roman Rig) are mysterious or enigmatic. The total length of this dyke is about 27 km. From north to south, the dyke begins in the outskirts of Sheffield, and follows the line of the Don valley to Kimberworth where it splits into two branches. One branch, the shorter one, goes to Swinton Common. The longer branch goes to Mexborough. The exact ends of the dyke are uncertain and there are a number of gaps in the monument which mean the exact route is unknown in parts. It is not known if any of these gaps are original or the result of later destruction. The form of the Roman Ridge is unique; no other dyke is known to have multiple branches. The Roman Ridge is first mentioned by Camden in his *Britannia* of 1586 and from the eighteenth century onwards the dyke was identified as a Roman road, for example by Joseph Hunter in his book *South Yorkshire* published in 1828.

The maximum height of the bank was about 2.5 m. The first full survey and description of the dyke was undertaken by Preston in 1949 (Preston), whose work is the basis of all subsequent work on the Roman Ridge. I will follow Preston's terminology and describe the branch leading to Mexborough as the north dyke and the one leading to Swinton Common as the south dyke. Preston believed the Roman Ridge was a single unified work, however it must be remembered that this is an assumption not a fact.

The dyke today is much eroded and flattened by agriculture and development. In two books – *Journey Along Roman Ridge* and *South-West Yorkshire's Roman Ridge, A Who Dug it Mystery* – K. A. Cronk exhaustively surveys the route of the Roman Ridge and all the possible routes it could take where there are no upstanding remains of the dyke.

The ends of the dyke are uncertain, at the Sheffield end there is no evidence of a dyke in the 2 km between Carwood Road and the Don. Here, just above the confluence of the Sheaf and the Don, was a major ford. Following the dyke from south to north, the next major problem is the relationship between the dyke and the Iron Age camp at Wincobank Hill. Unfortunately the dyke is not visible to the south of the hill and traces have been picked up again to the north of the hill. From excavations done by the South Yorkshire Archaeological Service it seems the dyke points towards Wincobank Hill and importantly no trace of the dyke was picked up on the line the dyke would have to take around the hill. Further along the dyke near the Blackburn valley a hoard of Roman coins was found in the nineteenth century. The hoard was described as coming from the dyke, which would confirm a pre-Roman date, most likely Iron Age, for its construction but the exact findspot is unknown.

On the Kimberworth Hills the exact route of the dyke is confused, which is a problem as it is here that the dyke splits into two. Interestingly the three branches of the Roman Ridge have several different names on the Kimberworth Hills; Danes Bank, Kemp Bank or Ditch, Roman Bank, Barber Balk and Scotland Balk. Here Preston and Greene's excavations in 1947 (Green and Preston, 'Two Excavations in the 'Roman Ridge' Dyke') showed the ditch was 1.8 m wide and 6.9 m deep and cut into the bedrock. The silting of the ditch had one fragment of Roman pottery. This was a fragment of mortarium of around AD 270. The twin dykes run along the edge of the Kimberworth Hills, not necessarily in the best place for defence and north of the Kimberworth Hills both dykes are overlooked by higher ground and the northern dyke runs into a ravine.

The southern branch of the dyke runs very close to the earthwork of Caesar's Camp, an earthwork which is most likely to be Iron Age in date. Again the relationship between the Roman Ridge and Caesar's Camp is unknown as the dyke is indistinct here and the line is inconclusive. The southern dyke seems to end in air and does not run down to the River Don. Hunter has the dyke terminating in a field, evidently dug away, he claimed. Cronk shows three possible continuations of the southern dyke, though none of them is particularly convincing as a defensive earthwork.

The northern dyke, like the southern arm of the Roman Ridge, disappears before reaching the Don at Mexborough. The northern dyke is generally less well preserved than the southern dyke but does have some impressive, well-preserved sections. Most of the northern dyke survives as low field boundaries, and here the line of the dyke is much more certain. The maximum dimensions of the northern dyke are a bank 2 m high, a ditch 2 m deep, with the combined width of bank and ditch being 13.5 m. Again the dyke has unexpected kinks and changes of direction and is overlooked by higher ground in some sections. The dyke as a defensive earthwork is not really convincing. There is no evidence that the dyke ran east through Mexborough to protect the ford at Strafford Sands across the Don.

Investigation of a possible entrance through the Roman Ridge in 1946 by Derek Riley showed that it was later than the ditch and not an original entrance (Riley). The ditch first silted quickly and then a second slower phase of filling. The ditch was 6–9 m wide and 1.25 m deep, while the bank was 4.5–6 m wide and 0.5 m high. No evidence of any re-cutting of the ditch was found.

Today the Roman Ridge appears as a discontinuous monument only surviving in woodland or where it was used as a field boundary. There appears to be no difference between land on one side or the other of the Rig and the land types between the dykes are too varied to be used for a single agricultural purpose. It seems the Roman Ridge acts as a boundary, not a natural line of defence. It is difficult to imagine that it could ever have been used a fortified or manned line of defence. Nicholas Boldrini notes (Boldrini) that all of the earlier studies of the Roman Ridge work on the assumption that the branches of the Roman Ridge were contemporary, which is not a certainty. Boldrini also makes the point that the area between the dykes may be as important at the dykes themselves. The liminal space between the dykes could be seen as a demilitarised zone or buffer space between two groups.

The Roman Ridge is going to have to remain on the uncertain list until further work provides a firm evidence of its construction date. However, the work done on the Scot's Dyke, the Aberford Dykes and the West Yorkshire Grim's Ditch make it more likely to be Iron Age in date instead of post-Roman. The Scot's Dyke and the Aberford Dykes show that very long dykes, with ditches cut into bedrock were constructed in Iron Age Yorkshire.

Wales and the Welsh Marches

Offa's Dyke

We can surmise that one spring around the year 787, Welshmen riding the cattle-rustling trails into Anglo-Saxon England came back with astonishing stories. Thousands of Anglo-Saxon levies had moved into the border country with horses and carts carrying rations, tents, rope, nails and weapons. But this time, unlike the mounted expeditions of so many previous years, they had not come to burn crops, seize goods and wield weapons of war: this year they had come to use tools – spades, axes, adzes and hammers. For they had been ordered to create a huge bank and ditch along the whole frontier – 25 feet deep, 60 feet

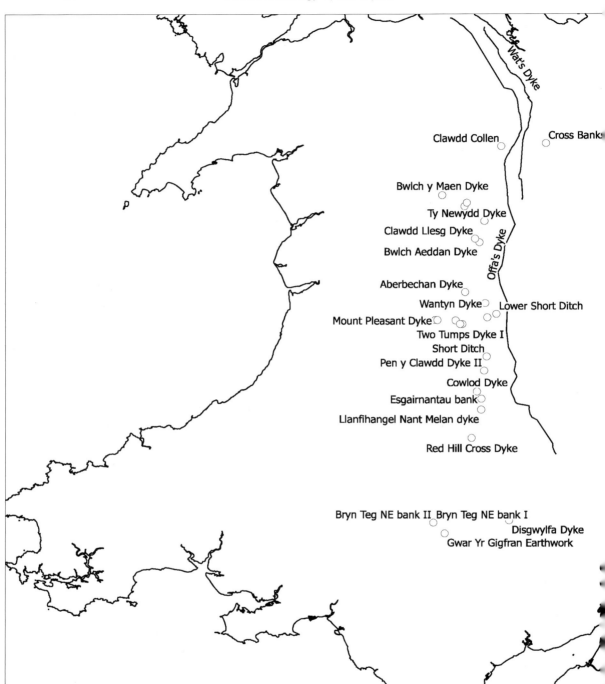

Clawdd Collen   Cross Bank

Bwlch y Maen Dyke

Ty Newydd Dyke

Clawdd Llesg Dyke

Bwlch Aeddan Dyke

Aberbechan Dyke

Wantyn Dyke   Lower Short Ditch

Mount Pleasant Dyke

Two Tumps Dyke I

Short Ditch

Pen y Clawdd Dyke II

Cowlod Dyke

Esgairnantau bank

Llanfihangel Nant Melan dyke

Red Hill Cross Dyke

Bryn Teg NE bank II Bryn Teg NE bank I

Disgwylfa Dyke

Gwar Yr Gigfran Earthwork

Map 23: Wales showing Offa's Dyke, Wat's Dyke and the Short Dykes.

across – from the Irish Sea to the Bristol Channel. Like modern motorway constructors they were to cut a swathe through the green countryside.

(Wood)

Offa's Dyke is different from the other post-Roman Dykes, because we know more about it than the other dykes and the questions usually asked are where and why it was built not who built it and when was it built. Offa, King of Mercia, is one of the few pre-Conquest Kings that most people have heard of, because of the massive dyke on the Welsh border that bears his name. The above description of the building of Offa's Dyke is what most people would believe – that it was built from the Bristol Channel to the north Wales coast and imposed as a border on the Welsh. As we shall see this description of the building of Offa's Dyke may be more imaginative fiction than known fact.

The scale of the Offa's Dyke is difficult to comprehend. If only the core part of the dyke, between Rushock Hill and Treuddyn, is counted it is 103 km long, 120 km long if the earthworks to the north and south are included as part of the dyke. Nothing else was built on this scale in Britain for a thousand years afterwards until the construction of turnpike roads and canals began in the eighteenth century. There are a number of questions about Offa's Dyke that need to be answered.

Was it really built by Offa of Mercia?

When exactly was Offa's Dyke built?

Was the Dyke imposed on the Welsh as a border without their consent?

Did Offa's Dyke really stretch from 'sea to sea'?

Was Offa's Dyke a defensive work or a just a boundary marker?

What is the relationship between Offa's Dyke and the related earthworks such as Wat's Dyke and the Short Dykes?

The first reference to the building of Offa's Dyke comes from Asser's Life of King Alfred.

There was in Mercia in fairly recent times, a certain vigorous king called Offa, who terrified all the neighbouring kings and provinces around him and who had a great dyke built between Wales and Mercia from sea to sea.

(Asser)

Asser was a monk who became Bishop of Sherborne around AD 890. His *Life of King Alfred* is the main source for Alfred's reign and the reference to Offa and Offa's Dyke is an aside. This is the only close contemporary reference we have to the building of a dyke and would be about a century after the construction of Offa's Dyke. There may be problems with this source as some scholars have claimed that the *Life of King Alfred* is a later medieval forgery and not the work of Asser, while others have strongly supported the authenticity of the *Life*. The only surviving manuscript of the *Life* was destroyed in a fire at the Cottonian Library in 1731 but fortunately a transcript had been made. This is not the place to discuss the sometimes complex arguments about the authenticity of *Life of King Alfred* but there are three possibilities:

Asser's life of Alfred is genuine and Offa of Mercia did build the dyke.

Asser's life is a forgery but is based on a genuine tradition that Offa built the dyke.

Asser's life is a forgery and Offa didn't build the dyke.

Whether the text is genuine or otherwise is not important except in case number three. Then the question arises why should the medieval forger assign the building of the dyke to King Offa? There is some separate evidence that Offa may have built the dyke that comes from the Anglo-Saxon poem Widsith.

Offa ruled Anglen ...

With his lone sword he defined a frontier against the Myrgingas at Fieldor

(S. A. Bradley)

This reference to an earlier King Offa of Anglen who defined a frontier may have inspired the eighth-century Offa of Mercia to emulate his namesake and possible ancestor to settle the frontier with the Welsh once and for all. Alternatively this poem could have been devised in praise of Offa of Mercia, showing him emulating the continental King Offa. The first reference we have to 'Offediche' does not occur until the thirteenth century in a document of a land grant near Rhiston in Shropshire.

The lack of historic references to Offa's Dyke is not surprising. We know very little about Mercia compared to other Anglo-Saxon kingdoms. The main source for this period, the Anglo-Saxon Chronicle, was composed in Wessex and is naturally strongly biased towards events in Wessex.

Yet precisely because Mercia eventually failed, its history remains obscure. Indeed, despite the kingdom's early political prominence there are virtually no Mercian written sources. Not only is there no Mercian chronicle but there was not even a single Mercian among the informants whom Bede consulted when preparing his Ecclesiastical History.

(Brooks)

Mercia means 'the people of the marches' or 'the boundary people'. The core area of Mercia seems to have been in the North Midlands. As Mercia expanded it incorporated a number of sub-kingdoms and groups of people such as Lindsey (modern Lincolnshire), the *Hwicce* (Worcestershire and Gloucestershire), the Pecsæte (people of the Peak district, north Derbyshire), the Wreocansæte (people of the Wrekin, north Shropshire) and the Magonsæte (Herefordshire and south Shropshire). At the height of Mercian power influence extended as far as London.

Offa was King of Mercia from AD 757 until AD 796. He came to the throne after deposing Beornred who had reigned only briefly after the assassination of King Aethelbald. We don't know the exact circumstances of Offa becoming King or how old he was, but he must have been a young man as he reigned for thirty-nine years. Offa was a Christian king, but he came into frequent conflict with the Church and its bishops.

Map 24: Offa's Dyke and the Mercian Frontier after Fox.

In the west Mercia bordered Wales which was divided into a number of princedoms. There was a pattern of shifting alliances between the Welsh and English kingdoms. Directly across the border in the north was the kingdom of Gwynedd, in the central marches was the largest kingdom of Powys and in the south was Gwent. The Welsh annals record a battle at Hereford in AD 760, Offa harrying Dyfed in AD 778 and an expedition into an unnamed part of Wales in AD 784. It is possible that Offa's Dyke dates to the period after AD 784 and before Offa's death in AD 796 when Offa decided to settle the border problem (Stenton).

Offa's Dyke was first mapped by John Speed in AD 1600. In the process he confused Wat's Dyke with Offa's Dyke, a confusion which continued to be shown on maps up to the nineteenth century. Offa's Dyke was first mapped in detail in the nineteenth century by the Ordnance Survey. This was not for archaeological research and included many dubious sections of the dyke but forms the basis of all subsequent work as many parts of the dyke shown by the Ordnance Survey have since been damaged or destroyed. The major archaeological fieldwork was done by Sir Cyril Fox in between 1926 and 1934 but he only did seven small excavations on the dyke.

Map 25: Offa's Dyke northern section after Fox.

Surprisingly no systematic excavation work was done between Fox in 1934 and the work done by David Hill and Margaret Worthington at Manchester University Extra-Mural Studies department in the 1970s. Hill & Worthington came to some radically different conclusions to Fox about the extent of Offa's Dyke. As there is a disagreement about which earthworks really belong to Offa's Dyke I will describe the whole of the dyke as described by Fox and then discuss some of the controversy about the extent of the dyke. Offa's Dyke falls into three sections which are:

The northern section from the sea near Prestatyn, Denbighshire, to Treuddyn, Flintshire.

The central section from Treuddyn to Rushock Hill, Herefordshire.

The southern section from Rushock Hill down the Wye Valley to the Severn.

The Northern Section

Between Treuddyn and Prestatyn there is 35.5 km of country where Fox found about 5.75 km of earthwork. Fox believed that the dyke was never finished here; because political and military effort was too weak in this area away from the Mercian heartlands.

There is a thirteenth-century reference to Offa's Dyke at Prestatyn but the reference is obscure and not easy to interpret. Prestatyn is an English place name, not recorded before the eleventh century but likely to be earlier. Meliden to the west is a Welsh name, so Fox put the border and therefore the dyke between these two places.

This detached section of the dyke is different from the central section of Offa's Dyke. The dyke is bivallate, with a ditch on both sides. At Brynbella a mound was incorporated into the dyke, possibly a Bronze Age burial mound. At Whitford there is a detached section of dyke known as the Whitford Dyke. This was accepted by Fox as being part of the line of the northern section of Offa's Dyke. At Ysceifiog Barrow the dyke runs up to the ditch round the barrow and starts again at the other side. This may indicate that the site was considered sacred and could not be damaged but also means that the dyke was not much use as a defensive earthwork here or even a way of controlling access, by leaving such an unfortified gap. There is a huge gap of 22.75 km between Treuddyn where the dyke starts again and the earthworks at Ysceifiog.

The Central Section, Treuddyn to Rushock Hill

Treuddyn in Flintshire is agreed to be the northernmost part of the main stretch of Offa's Dyke. It stretches for 103 km of almost continuous earthwork. From Treuddyn southwards, the dyke is almost a straight line, running along the edge of the uplands. The dyke runs down one side of a steep valley and will run straight up the other side. Preservation is better on the high ground and the dyke usually with a single ditch on the west side is still an impressive monument. In the lower part of the valleys the dyke has been ploughed down or destroyed. One section of the dyke has a ditch on the east side of the bank. At several points streams have been diverted into the ditch, either to prevent them from eroding the bank or to make a more difficult obstacle. The ditch is V-shaped and cut into the limestone bedrock in places. The overall breadth of bank and ditch is up to 19.5 m. The bank stands up to 2.3 m high and ditch 2.1 m deep.

In north Shropshire the dyke has suffered more damage by agriculture and building work, especially the construction of trackways through the dyke. On the upland sections there is a lack of gaps in the dyke, which Fox claimed showed the purpose of the Dyke was built to prevent uncontrolled movement, and only allow movement by controlled routes.

The dyke is sited to get maximum visual control over the Marches. From some viewpoints the dyke can be seen for miles running across the countryside. In some other places it does not occupy the high ground or take the shortest route. There is

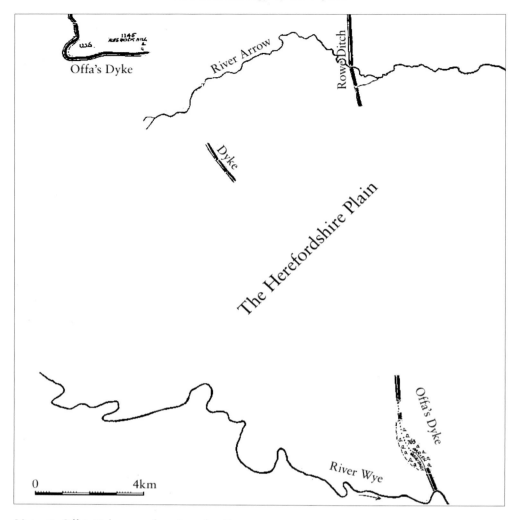

Map 26: Offa's Dyke central section after Fox.

a spur on which Pen y Gardden hillfort is situated. It is excluded from the dyke and overlooks it. It is possible that this fort was under Welsh control.

The dyke then crosses into the lower ground of the valley of the River Vyrnwy and River Severn. From the River Vyrnwy to the Severn Offa's Dyke is very straight. The dyke runs to the River Severn at Severn Howe. There is a gap from here to Buttington, where the River Severn possibly forms the boundary and the built dyke recommences at Buttington on Severn.

In the mountain zone of south Shropshire and Powys between the River Teme and the Lugg valley the highest point of Offa's Dyke is reached at Hawthorn Hill at 396 m. Again here there is a section of dyke with an eastern ditch. The hillforts of Castle Ring and Burfa Camp, in Powys, are used to align the dyke. At Hergan Hill the dyke makes a right-angled bend which Fox believed shows two construction techniques meeting, one with a counterscarp bank, and the other without a counterscarp. Again the dyke disappears in the valleys, possibly because of ploughing, for example across the Clun valley there are no traces of the dyke in the alluvial soil. The central section of Offa's Dyke ends on Rushock Hill in Herefordshire.

The Southern Section in the Wye Valley

The dyke only exists in fragments here; the dyke is more gap than earthwork. Fox accepts this as being part of a continuing Offa's Dyke. From Rushock Hill, Herefordshire to Holme Marsh the dyke is traceable but not continuous, here Fox claims that gaps were blocked by 'jungle'. Then there is a large gap of 8 km then some discontinuous earthworks on a line to the River Wye. South of this point Fox claims the Wye was used as the boundary. This area has Old Red Sandstone as the underlying geology and Fox makes his usual argument that it was heavily forested and there was no need for a dyke here.

English Bicknor in Gloucestershire is where the earthworks are seen again. At Symonds Yat, earthworks across the loop of the Wye may have been incorporated into the dyke but are Iron Age in date. The Gloucestershire section of the dyke is more irregular with some sections having a west ditch while others have an eastern one to provide material for the bank. At Sedbury Cliff Offa's Dyke stops on the cliffs above the River Severn.

Fox divides Offa's Dyke into three types of construction:

Type I sections – built straight in a straight line from A to B.
Type II sections – direct line from A to B but sinuous.
Type III – A to B has no direct alignment, the dyke follows the contours.

Fox suggests that Type II sections were originally set out in thick woodland where straight lines were difficult to mark out. There was some correlation between type II sections and the 1920s woodland. Type I sections were set out on more open ground where it was easier to layout a straight line. Fox uses the Type I and II division to map the open and forested land along the dyke in the eighth century.

To sum up Fox's argument: Offa's Dyke did stretch from sea to sea as Asser had claimed. Also Offa's Dyke was the work of one person who had the responsibility for selecting the line of the dyke, who is referred to as 'The Engineer'. The dyke was not unilaterally imposed on the Welsh but was a negotiated boundary, shown by deflections from the straight line of the dyke due to land being held by the Welsh or English. Offa's Dyke was not a manned defence but it was an obstacle to movement, and was used to channel movement through certain points only. It was as much a struggle against nature as against the Welsh.

It demonstrates the competence, skill, and dogged determination applied through two centuries to the solution of a difficult problem by related groups of English-men in the Dark Ages; and the reality and vigour of the Welsh opposition which made such efforts necessary. It also helps us to see, though in blurred outline, one corner of a lost England, the England of the Anglo-Saxon pioneer, adventurer, frontiersman. Here, on the borders

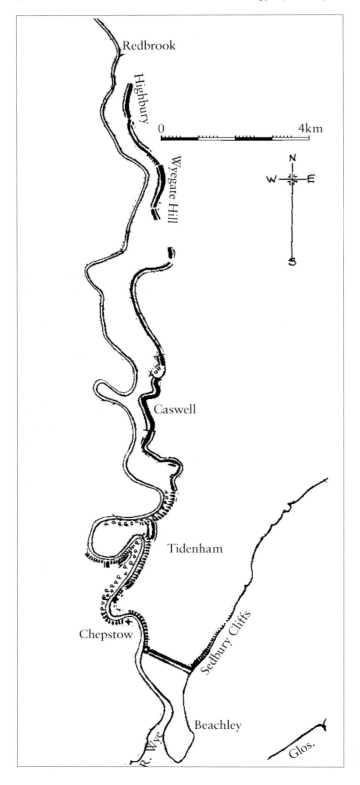

Map 27: Offa's Dyke
southern section after Fox.

of the highland, nature was his enemy as well as man. Densely forested hills, ravines matted with primeval jungle, extensive and impassable marshes environed his ways and conditioned his activities, agricultural and military.

(C. Fox, *Offa's Dyke*)

It was not until the renewed excavation work on Offa's Dyke from the 1970s onwards that this view of Offa's Dyke was seriously challenged. Over a period of thirty years David Hill and Margaret Worthington have carried out dozens of small excavations along the line of Offa's Dyke (Hill & Worthington, *Offa's Dyke History and Guide*). This has lead to a different interpretation of Offa's Dyke to Cyril Fox's. They reject Fox's explanation that any gaps are filled with forest and it is shown to be wrong in at least one place where Fox's 'primeval forest' is caused by nineteenth-century landscaping. For example the 90-degree turn at Hergan Bank that Fox claimed was a spot where different gangs met is interpreted by them as being caused by the dyke holding to the line of the contour. At several places where Fox had claimed that a gap in the dyke was original they showed that the dyke had once existed. Controversially they claim that the northern and southern sections of the dyke, as described above, do not actually exist. Fox was misled by the Royal Commission's Inventory of Flintshire into identifying miscellaneous earthworks as a northward continuation of Offa's Dyke, and that the earthworks in Herefordshire and Gloucestershire have nothing to do with Offa's Dyke. They criticise Fox for leaving no 'school' of dyke studies and also quote Frank Noble that Fox left a 'dead monument in a dead landscape'.

In the northern section a number of excavations on the supposed line of Offa's Dyke failed to find any evidence of it ever having existed. Hill & Worthington see two short complete earthworks between Treuddyn and the sea, one around the Yscefiog Barrow and the other on the Brynbella barrow. They strongly suggest that these are two Bronze Age earthworks but there is no dating evidence from excavation. The Whitford Dyke is a medieval boundary and a separate monument unconnected with Offa's Dyke. Somewhat pedantically Hill & Worthington also point out that the Whitford Dyke stops at Prestatyn 5 km short of the sea, so even if it was part of Offa's Dyke it would not have stretched from sea to sea.

They also believe that Offa's Dyke stops at Rushock Hill and the southern section does not exist on the Herefordshire Plain or in Gloucestershire. The earthworks on the Herefordshire Plain are slight and have huge gaps, a greater amount of gap than earthwork in fact. The Gloucestershire earthworks are not connected with Offa's Dyke at all because here they have a ditch on the east side. Hill & Worthington suggest a number of possibilities about Offa's Dyke south of Rushock Hill:

The line of Offa's Dyke on the Herefordshire Plain has been destroyed by agriculture.

The Rowe Ditch and other earthworks on the Herefordshire Plain formed part of the line of Offa's Dyke.

Gaps in the dyke were filled by a palisade or by felled trees.

The dyke stopped at Rushock Hill.

They strongly support the last possibility. Their model of the dyke is of a defended border, not a negotiated line of settlement. The dyke protected by regular patrols, possibly mounted, along the line of the dyke with defended villages and possibly beacons on high points set back from the dyke with a zone of cleared forest in front of the dyke. The dyke is the border between Mercia and Powys, not Mercia and Wales as a whole.

There are some problems with this model. The evidence for a patrolled dyke is slight and Offa's Dyke does make some odd deviations from the most defensible line which is difficult to explain if it is a purely defensive earthwork. Also the Gloucestershire sections cannot be dismissed as not being part of Offa's Dyke because of the east-facing ditch. As we have seen there are sections of Offa's Dyke in the central marches that have an eastern ditch as well. Also there is a reference to 'Offedich' in Gloucestershire as early as AD 1321 in St Briavels parish (Currie, Herbert & Baggs).

Hill & Worthington have their own fixed ideas about Offa's Dyke as much as Fox does. Offa's Dyke is seen as a uniform monument and must have a west-facing ditch like the central section throughout. This is as much a preconception as Fox's idea of a dyke from sea to sea with forest filled gaps. The small-scale excavations of the last thirty years have left more questions than answers. While the existence of the dyke has been confirmed or disproved at several points the full extent of Offa's Dyke is still uncertain. The evidence that the earthworks of Offa's Dyke did not extend further north than Treuddyn is at present much stronger than the evidence that it did not extend further south than Rushock Hill. The early references to 'Offedich' in Gloucestershire must be explained away somehow if the dyke did not extend to here. If Offa's Dyke did have gaps filled with a palisade or some other boundary marker this would strengthen the idea of a negotiated frontier as opposed to a defended boundary. The relationship between Offa's Dyke and the other dykes in the region becomes more important. This will be discussed in the next section.

Wat's Dyke

One of the puzzling features of Offa's Dyke is its relationship with Wat's Dyke. Wat's Dyke extends from the Dee Estuary near Holywell to Maesbury Hill in north Shropshire, a distance of 62 km. There was early confusion between Wat's Dyke and Offa's Dyke, with references to Offa's Dyke terminating at Basingwerk. This should refer to Wat's Dyke. Basingwerk is 'the fort of the people of Bassa' and may refer to a fortified place close to the end of Wat's Dyke. There are also three farms located on Wat's Dyke called Bryn Offa, Llwyn Offa and Clawdd Offa. When these farms were named is unknown.

Wat's Dyke is referred to in early documents as Clawdd Wade, Clawdd Wode and Clawdd Wad, from the Anglo-Saxon Wada or Wade. Wada is mentioned in Widsith as the ruler of the Hælsinga who lived between the Eider and the Elbe. He is mentioned in other Germanic tales as a sea giant. Keith Fitzpatrick-Mathews has pointed out in Britain, besides Wat's Dyke, there is a Wade's Causeway – the Roman road between Malton and Whitby, Wade's Gap along Hadrian's Wall, and Wade's Stone; one each at Barnaby and Goldsborough in North Yorkshire, which preserve his name. By the twelfth century Wade is referred to as Gado and described as a son of the king of the

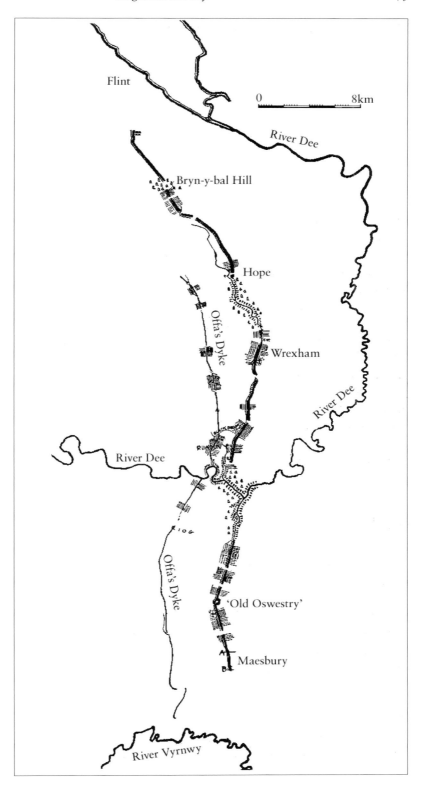

Map 28: Wat's
Dyke after Fox.

Vandals and a friend of Offa of Mercia who helped him fight off the Romans. It seems that by this time Offa and Wade were firmly linked. This may show that the dykes were seen to have a common origin, at least by the high Middle Ages.

Wat's Dyke and Offa's Dyke run an approximately parallel course, and at Ruabon they are very close together. The whole of Wat's Dyke runs at a much lower elevation than Offa's Dyke, along the lowlands. At Holywell there are traces of the dyke much damaged by nineteenth-century development. There are a few more detached sections of dyke in Wern Sirk wood but not until Coed-Llys does the dyke reappear as a visible earthwork. The dyke is now mostly continuous except for some small gaps caused by development and agriculture. The exception is a gap of 5.6 km from Bryn y gaer to a loop of the River Alun. Fox claims the Ordnance Survey map is incorrect here and the marked line of Wat's Dyke is just a hedge bank and the River Alun forms the boundary line here.

As Wat's Dyke passes through Wrexham it is mostly destroyed but there are some surprisingly substantial sections of the dyke surviving. The dyke runs into and uses the earthworks of the hillfort at Yr Hên Ddinas (Old Oswestry) as part of its line. In the line up to the River Morda the dyke is badly damaged by the erosion of the stream. The Morda appears to be canalised for 4 km and used as an extension of Wat's Dyke but then stops. No more traces of earthworks are found further south. Wat's Dyke is laid out in straight sections from one landmark to the next and links a number of Iron Age hillforts such as Old Oswstry.

For Fox 'the work is a unity, the creation of one mind, the projection of one will' designed by a man trained in a military tradition. Also the dyke was never completed, political and military effort faded out in the north-west and the gaps in the dyke at the northern end are natural. Fox thought Wat's Dyke predated Offa's Dyke, being the work of Aethelbald, Offa's predecessor while Hill & Worthington were agnostic on the relationship between the two dykes. Fox as usual assumed forest filled the existing gaps in Wat's Dyke, but Hill's excavations has shown the existence of the ditch in three of these gaps (Hill, 'Offa's & Wat's Dykes').

In 1997 an excavation at Mile Oak, Shropshire gave a single radiocarbon date of AD 411–561 for a hearth found sealed beneath the dyke (Hannaford). Misinterpretations of this date lead to suggestions that Wat's Dyke was a post-Roman British construction and was probably built by the successor community to the *civitas* of the Cornovii. The radiocarbon date did not refer to the construction of the dyke, but to the hearth which could have been out of use for centuries before Wat's Dyke was built.

Excavations in 2006 (Hayes and Malim) in advance of road building south of Gobowen in Shropshire gave an opportunity for OSL and radiocarbon dating to be used on samples from Wat's Dyke to see if firmer dates could be obtained. The excavation showed that Wat's Dyke had a marker bank set out first to show the line of the bank, formed from earth taken from deturfing the ditch and a cobblestone spread used as a foundation for the bank. The ditch was V-shaped with an 'ankle breaker' slot in the base, like Roman military earthworks. The ditch was 6–8 m wide and up to 4 m deep, with a bank on the eastern side 8 m wide and up to 1.5 m high. White stones were possibly used to mark the line of the bank and the bank was built in a single phase. At Gobowen the preservation of environmental remains was poor, so no evidence of past environment was recovered.

The results of the OSL dating suggest that the fills of the dyke are ninth century AD. This suggests that Wat's Dyke post-dates Offa's Dyke and was built when the Mercian frontier was threatened by a resurgent kingdom of Powys under Cyngen or his successor Rhodri Mawr. Wat's Dyke is more defensible than Offa's Dyke, which lies on the higher and remoter ground. Wat's Dyke overlaps Offa's Dyke but also stretches to the Flintshire coast. This may suggest danger from Gwynedd as well as Powys at this time. Offa's Dyke can be seen as a political frontier controlling access between Mercia and Powys while Wat's Dyke more of a defensive line, built to strengthen a border becoming more troubled.

The Short Dykes

In addition to Offa's Dyke and Wat's Dyke there are a whole series of other dykes on the Welsh Marches. There are groups of dykes on the Shropshire hills, the Glamorgan uplands, in Herefordshire and in Powys. They range in size from the Wantyn Dyke, 3 km long to the Shepherd's Well dyke only 100 m long. Most of the dykes are single bank and ditch, but others have multiple banks and ditches like cross-ridge dykes of southern England.

Fox considered as a 'working hypothesis' that some of them were precursors of Offa's Dyke, built to prevent incursions from north Wales. For example the Short Ditches on the Kerry Hills were Mercian defences prior to Offa. Fox's scheme was simple, the short dykes range in date for a hundred years from the mid-seventh century onwards, were succeeded by Wat's Dyke and then rendered obsolete by Offa's Dyke. The short dykes reflect the ebb and flow of the English conquest. In contrast Hill & Worthington considered the Short Dykes as disparate group, not a unified set of monuments, and ranging from prehistoric to Tudor in date.

The most important of the Short Dykes includes:

Clawdd Mawr in Powys
Crugyn Bank
The Upper Short Ditch
The Giant's Grave
The Short Ditch
Double Deyches
Wantyn Dyke

All the short ditches are sited at the western end of a fertile valley and block access from the west. There are also three earthworks in Herefordshire that are also possibly Anglo-Saxon. The earthworks at Yatton Wood and Perrystone Court Fox regarded as a 'Magonsæton' work, built by the people who lived in Herefordshire and south Shropshire, and not part of Offa's Dyke, but they have not been excavated so their dates have not been confirmed. The Rowe Ditch is a substantial monument to the east of Pembridge in Herefordshire. It is about 3.5 km long with a ditch on the western side and is cut by the River Arrow. The Rowe Ditch lies over a ditch, which has been partly excavated and produced Iron Age and Roman pottery, supporting the idea that the Rowe Ditch is Anglo-Saxon in date. It has sometimes has been considered as a second alignment of Offa's Dyke (Rodd). However, if Offa's Dyke does not extend across the Herefordshire Plain then the Rowe Ditch would be the main boundary here.

The problem was there was no dating of any of the short dykes and subsequently it was suggested that at least some of them were prehistoric in date. The excavation of two linear earthworks on Ratlinghope and Stitt Hill, Shropshire suggested they were prehistoric by analogy with sites in Southern England though no dating evidence was found (Guilbert). This was strengthened by the radiocarbon dates from the Devil's Mouth Dyke near Church Stretton, which gave radiocarbon dates of the mid to late Bronze Age.

In 2001 the Clwyd-Powys Archaeological Trust began a program of auguring and excavation of the short dykes (Hankinson & Caseldine). There are at least twenty examples in Powys. Fourteen dykes were augured in total and five dykes produced peat or charred material for radiocarbon dating. The samples were from Clawdd Mawr, Crugyn Bank, the Upper Short Ditch, the Giants' Grave and the (lower) Short Ditch.

Site	Date 1 Standard Deviation
Lower Short Ditch	cal. AD 410–590
Giant's Grave	AD 340–530
Upper Short Ditch	AD 540–660
Crugyn Bank	AD 650–780
Clawdd Mawr	AD 630–710

The calibrated dates were all early medieval. The Giant's Grave has an earlier date than the other dykes but the dating was on a sample of peat not charcoal like the other dykes. This confirms Fox's dating for at least these dykes, if not all of the Welsh Short Dykes, but the idea that they were Anglo-Saxon works has not been confirmed. The relationship between the Short Dykes, Wat's Dyke and Offa's Dyke is still uncertain. All the sites have weaknesses as defensive structures. Hankinson & Caseldine suggest that instead of being defensive each dyke marked the boundaries of a *cantref*; an early Welsh territory. Half of all the known dykes in Powys lie within one kilometre of putative *cantref* boundaries.

This survey has shown that the number of dykes that can be definitely assigned to the post-Roman period is not a great as once thought. The Wansdyke, the Cambridgeshire Dykes, the Grey Ditch, the Pear Wood Grim's Dyke, the Fossditch, Bokerley Dyke, the Welsh Short Dykes, Wat's Dyke and of course Offa's Dyke are all certainly post-Roman. Comb's Ditch and the *Fullingadic* and the *Faestendic* are in the likely post-Roman category. Other dykes may be of this period but we don't have any firm evidence about them. These possible post-Roman dykes are listed in the gazetteer.

CHAPTER 3

THE ORIGIN OF THE DYKES – ROMAN, BRITISH OR GERMANIC?

Who Built the Dykes?

Offa's Dyke and Wat's Dyke are Mercian constructions while the Short Dykes are likely to have been built by the Welsh. Where did the use of dykes as boundary markers or defences originate from? There are three main possibilities. One is that they were originally built by the native Romano-British population following example of the Iron Age Dykes that still existed in the landscape around them. Another possibility is that they were built by the Romano-British or Anglo-Saxons following the example of Roman frontier works such as Hadrian's Wall and the Antonine Wall. The final possibility is that they are based on similar monuments from Denmark and Germany, the homeland of the Anglo-Saxons.

Who built the dykes links into the question of when were they built? One idea is that the dykes began to be built in the period immediately after the end of Roman political control, marking the boundaries of several of the civitates as Roman power vanished. Alternatively the dykes could also mark out the territories of later rulers as British kingdoms emerged out of the ruins of Britannia. In both these cases the dykes would be built by the native Romano-British population against other Romano-British groups.

Another possibility is that the dykes were started in a later period. Once the Anglo-Saxons had established their territories, the dykes were used to mark the boundaries between the British and the Anglo-Saxons. An alternative is that they were built at a still later period and mark the boundaries between the emerging Anglo-Saxon kingdoms as they competed for territory and political control and only later as the dykes were used to mark the border with Wales. In this case they would be built by the Anglo-Saxon population. Of course all of these explanations may be correct and building dykes was a common solution to the problem of boundary marking that was constantly being repeated over a period of two centuries or more, between rival groups, and the Anglo-Saxons or Romano-British commonly both had a tradition of building earthworks.

Prehistoric Linear Earthworks

The most obvious forerunner of the post-Roman dykes are the large number of defensive and agricultural dykes that were built in the centuries before the Roman invasion. By the Bronze Age increasing population and climate change caused more pressure on agricultural land. From about 1700 BC the landscape of Britain began to be divided up by stone walls, ditches and dykes.

There are a number of short dykes up to 1 km long that survive in uplands across England known as cross dykes, cross-ridge dykes and spur dykes.

The taxonomy of these dykes was developed in the early part of the twentieth century by, among others, Cecil Curwin and Williams-Freeman. Williams-Freeman categorised these earthworks into cross-ridge dykes and spur dykes. Cross-ridge dykes run across downland between the heads of opposing valleys while spur dykes cross a spur between the edges of two adjacent valleys. Cross-ridge dykes can be bivallate, univallate, single or multiple ditches while spur dykes are univallate with a bank on the downhill side. Curwin believed that cross-ridge dykes were really covered trackways.

As Bradley (R. Bradley, 'Stock raising and the origins of the hillfort on the South Downs') has pointed out this classification is based on examples in Sussex and may not be applicable elsewhere, for example in Wessex (P. J. Fowler, 'Cross Dykes on the Ebble-Nadder Ridge'). Also Curwen's theory of cross-ridge dykes being covered ways and spur dykes being toll barriers is also untenable. It is likely that the bivallate dykes were territorial barriers. The distinction between cross-ridge dykes and spur dykes has been ignored by English Heritage for their Monuments Protection Program and all these dykes have been grouped together as cross dykes.

There are also longer linear dykes from 1 to 10 km long. These linear earthworks or linear ditches are also known as ranch boundaries, which start to be built around the end of the early Bronze Age, and continue to be built into the late Iron Age. Linear ditches seem to be used to mark out agricultural blocks of land, especially marking out pastoral from arable soil. Up to 10 km long they are straight only in short sections, they kink (to respect existing features?) and make bends at right angles. Their general form is sinuous. Gaps in the earthworks of up to 100 m seem to be original features of the monument. The dyke banks may be single or multiple, with banks on either up or down slope of the monument and banks may change sides in the course of the monument. Palisades on one or both sides of the dyke are known. All seem to be part of bigger systems of earthworks, they don't appear in isolation. One example is the Cleave Dyke system which lies on the western part of the Hambledon Hills in North Yorkshire. There are 9 km of banks and ditches, much of which is now destroyed. The system runs along the western scarp of the Hambledon Hills, with several dykes running at right angles to the main Cleave Dyke. The main Cleave Dyke incorporates and cuts through several round barrows so it must post-date the late Bronze Age.

As the name 'ranch boundary' suggests they seem to represent an increase in the pastoral economy. Whether this was the replacement of arable agriculture with stock rearing or the tighter integration of the two systems due to increased pressure on land due to climate change or population pressure is a subject of dispute. The distribution of linear earthworks covers Wessex (Hampshire, Dorset and Berkshire), Bedfordshire, north-east Yorkshire, the Yorkshire Wolds, and Cumbria. It is not known whether this pattern is the result of differential survival of monuments on the chalk uplands (English Heritage) or a real regional distribution.

In addition to these long agricultural dykes, there are defensive or territorial dykes around *Oppida*. *Oppidum* (pl. *oppida*) is an awkward term. Julius Caesar applied the term to settlements in Gaul and Britain. The proto-urban settlements of Gaul, with evidence of town planning are unlike the large areas of agricultural land and occupation enclosed by linear earthworks in southern Britain. The term 'territorial oppida' is sometimes used instead for British examples. The best known and studied sites are at Colchester (Camulodunum) and St Albans (Verulamium).

Around the Iron Age settlement at Colchester there is a complex of sixteen dykes (Hawkes & Crummy, 'Colchester Archaeological Report 11: Camulodunum 2'). The Colchester Dykes are also known as the Lexden Dykes. The westernmost dyke is known as Gryme's Dyke. In the thirteenth century Gryme's Dyke was still used as a marker, to mark the boundary of the Liberty of Colchester (Hawkes and Hull, Camulodunum). As Colchester is situated on a peninsular, with rivers to the north and south, the dykes to the west cut off access and make the peninsular defensible. The later dykes ignored the contours and were straighter than the earlier ones. There were some traces of a revetment for some of the dykes but no indication of any palisades on the top. It seems that the purpose of the dykes was to protect different areas within Colchester. 'It was built like an obstacle-course with different lines of defence, each giving those under attack time to retreat and regroup or flee' (Hawkes & Crummy, 'Colchester Archaeological Report 11: Camulodunum 2').

Most of the area inside the *oppidum* was not occupied, but two areas Gosbecks and Sheepen seem to have been heavily occupied. Sheepen was an area of trade and manufacturing while Gosbecks was more agricultural in character. The earthworks developed over a long period of time and seemed to have continued in use into the early Roman period.

At St Albans there is a similar situation, there are two main Iron Age boundary dykes. The Devil's Dyke covers the approach to Verulamium from the north across the valley of the River Ver. A second dyke, the Beach Bottom Dyke is 2.4 km long and is situated to the north-east of Verulamium. Wheeler (Wheeler & Wheeler) shows the dyke marks off the chalk land from heavier clay soil. The Beach Bottom Dyke presumably marked the northern boundary of Verulamium between the valleys of the Ver and the Lea. To the north-east another Devil's Dyke marks the boundary of another *oppidum* at Wheathampstead, presumably the predecessor to the *oppidum* at Verulamium. The *oppidum* at Verulamium is protected by a series of linear dykes in the area known as Prae Wood. New evidence from aerial photography has added the complexity of this earthwork system since Wheeler's publication (Hunn).

Ireland

It is useful to look at the Ireland to see how the dykes developed in an area outside of Roman political control. There are a number of linear earthworks in Ireland. The main monuments include the Black Pig's Dyke, the Dane's Cast, the Duncla and the Worm Ditch. There is also the earthwork known as the Dorsey which is associated with the linear earthwork of the Black Pig's Dyke, whose status is uncertain; either an enclosure or a complex of linear earthworks. Even today myths about the Irish dykes persist. At the beginning of *A History of Ulster*, Jonathan Bardon uses the 'defensive wall' which marked off Ulster fully two millennia ago as a metaphor:

> Described on maps as the Dane's Cast, it begins in the east near Scarva on the Down-Armagh border; the next section, known as the Dorsey, stands at Drummill Bridge in south Armagh; it continues into Monaghan near Muckno Lake, where it is known either as the Worm Ditch or as the Black Pig's Dyke; and further short stretches extend through Cavan and Fermanagh to Donegal Bay. A tradition survives that it was ploughed up by the tusks of an enchanted black boar; archaeologists, however, have proved this great linear earthwork to have been a series of massive defences, not continuous, but guarding the routeways into Ulster between the bogs, loughs and drumlins.
>
> (Bardon)

This ultimately derives from the work on the Black Pig's Dyke by W. F. de Vismes Kane (Kane, 'The black pig's dyke: the ancient boundary fortification of Uladh' and Kane, 'Additional Researches on the Black Pig's Dyke'). The Black's Pig's Dykes is in County Monaghan and is also known as the Black Pig's Race, or Black Pig's Race Rut or Black Pig's Race Valley. Kane described the legend of the black pig, a magical animal from Meath that tore up the course of the dyke with its snout. Kane's method may be gathered from this quote, in his typically verbose and wordy prose style.

> we may here lay down the general position that in estimating the general relationship or connection with each other of the fragmentary remains still extant, it is reasonable to conclude that if detached portions of such works show a similar plan and section, allowing a certain latitude for deviation and adaption where the contour of the ground suggests it; and present a unity of design in regards to some definite frontier demarcation of which we have historic testimony, we shall be justified in concluding that these separate links are portions of a once complete frontier line.
>
> (Kane, 'The black pig's dyke: the ancient
> boundary fortification of Uladh')

Kane draws parallels with the Wansdyke in Britain which he claims is a 'Belgic' work. Any gaps in this expanded Black Pig's Dyke were assumed to be the result of destruction by agriculture or were natural gaps as the result of mountain, forest or bog. However there is little evidence that these missing sections ever existed. In final form Kane's Black

Pig's Dyke was about 209 km long, stretching completely across Ireland. Kane claims the Black Pig's Dyke as the historic boundary of the kingdom of Ulster and specifically dates the dyke to the period AD 130–160. Kane's sections of the Black Pig's Dyke and the Worm's Cast are sometimes bivallate and sometimes univallate. In some areas the dyke is overlooked from both sides. The Black Pig's Dyke is to be a collection of disparate linear earthworks, some substantial, but unlikely ever to have been a continuous barrier.

The Dorsey is a large earthwork which has been described as 'a unique and intriguing site' (C. J. Lynn, 'Excavations at the Dorsey, County Armagh, 1977') and which adjoins part of the Black Pig's Dyke. The relationship between the two monuments is uncertain. Kane thought it was attached to the dyke. There has been some discussion as to what the Dorsey actually is. Work in the 1930s and 1940s by Davies (Davies, 'Excavations on the Dorsey and Black Pig's Dyke') assumed that the Dorsey and the Black Pig's Dyke were linked and that they were inspired by Roman frontier works and so must be later than the second century AD. As the Dorsey was detached from the Black Pig's Dyke Davies assumed that it was copying Roman forts as seen from the outside of the frontier.

> The constructional idea may be Roman; but the execution is thoroughly un-Roman and unpractical, the enclosure being placed wholly in advance of the frontier line. Some forts on Hadrian's Wall project slightly; and the planning of the Dorsey suggests and acquaintance with Roman lines of defence solely from the outside.
>
> (Davies, 'Excavations on the Dorsey and Black Pig's Dyke')

If it is an enclosure the Dorsey is unique in Ireland. It has been suggested its function was to pen cattle stolen in raids. It has also been reinterpreted as a series of linear earthworks (C. J. Lynn, 'The Dorsey and other linear earthworks'). The Dorsey lies on the road from Newtownhamilton to Dundalk, an ancient route from Louth to Armagh or to Navan Fort. Navan Fort is identified with Emhain Macha the ancient capital of Ulster. As Dorsey is Irish for door or gate it has been suggested that the Dorsey barred the road to the Emhain Macha. This route is also barred by a section of the Dane's Cast, 6.4 km south of Armagh city. The fortunate discovery of preserved timbers from the Dorsey showed the timbers were felled around the decade of 140 BC, contemporary with the main building at Navan Fort.

The Dane's Cast (also spelt as Danes Cast) forms the boundary of County Down and County Armagh. It is a discontinuous earthwork over 16 km long, interrupted by bog in several places. The dyke runs just below the hilltop, with a ditch on the up side of the slope, except for the northern end of the earthwork where the bank is between two ditches. This is unlikely to be a defensive earthwork, more like an agricultural boundary, and does appear similar to dykes such as the Chiltern Grim's Ditch. The Irish name is Gleann na Muice duibhe, the glen of the Black Pig. It is not sure when the name Dane's Cast was first used for this monument.

The Irish dykes provide some interesting comparisons to the English dykes. There are similar problems of trying to interpret them by linking them to historic or proto-historic events. There is also a similar tendency to join unrelated sections of earthworks together to create immense monuments of single date and purpose. The dykes are Iron Age but there is no evidence for when they went out of use. The Dane's Cast was used a county boundary but it is unknown whether it was still in use or just a convenient marker to use when the county boundary was set out.

Similarly there are many of linear earthworks in Scotland but nearly all are undated. The two major dykes that have been claimed as being of Dark Age date are the Deil's Dyke Galloway and the Caitrail in the Borders. The Deil's Dyke is discussed in the appendix.

Linear Defences in Britain and the Roman World

Roman military engineers had a long tradition of building linear defences in earthwork. For example in 58 BC, during his Gallic campaign, Julius Caesar learned that the Helvetii were planning a mass migration and intending to move through Roman territory. While Caesar talked to their ambassadors he also made preparations:

> In the meantime he employed the legion he had with him, and the troops that had been raised in the Province, to fortify the bank of the Rhone for a distance of eighteen miles between the Lake of Geneva and the Jura, the frontier between the Helvetii and the Sequani. This was effected by means of a rampart sixteen feet high with a trench running parallel. He then placed redoubts at intervals along the fortification and garrisoned them with pickets, so that he could stop the Helvetii more easily, should they attempt to force a passage.
>
> (Caesar, *The Conquest of Gaul*)

This wall, 30 km long and 4.8 m high, was intended to prevent a force of 300,000 (according to Caesar) migrating across the Rhone. This is not an isolated example of Roman skill at building large earthwork defences. During the siege of Alesia in 52 BC, Caesar's troops constructed a line of circumvallation round Alesia, about 18 km long and 4 m high. This presumably was an earth wall. This wall was strengthened by two inner ditches each 4.5 m wide and 4.5 m deep and the inner ditch was flooded to provide a more difficult obstacle. This formidable barrier was further strengthened by the addition of a rampart with a timber wall 4 m high, with the addition of projecting stakes cut to a point. There were also covered pits containing stakes and iron hooks in front of the rampart. To protect his besieging troops, Caesar also ordered the construction of a line of contravallation, outward facing, 21 km long. This whole series of fortifications was constructed in less than two months.

About a century after Caesar the Romans invaded Britain permanently. At first only the southern part of Britain was under direct Roman control, with a series of client kingdoms under friendly rulers around the borders. Gradually due to a combination of ambitious governors and native revolts the area of the province of Britannia was extended, the Romans were drawn deeper into Britain and the frontier pushed forward.

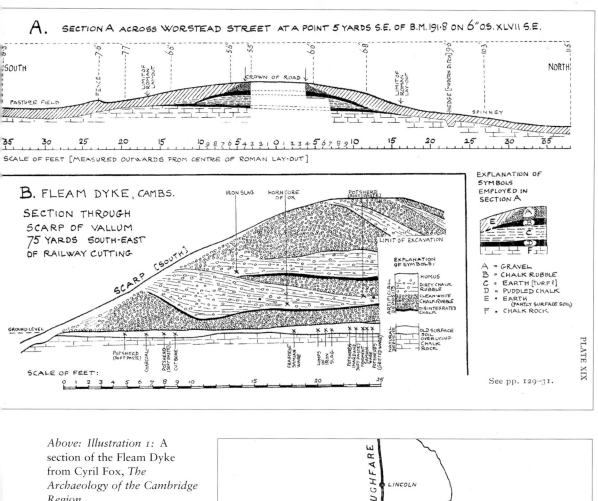

A. SECTION A ACROSS WORSTEAD STREET AT A POINT 5 YARDS S.E. OF B.M. 191·8 ON 6" O.S. XLVII S.E.

SOUTH

NORTH

FENCE
LIMIT OF ROMAN LAYOUT
CROWN OF ROAD
LIMIT OF ROMAN LAY-OUT
HEDGE [MODERN DITCH]
SPINNEY
PASTURE FIELD

SCALE OF FEET [MEASURED OUTWARDS FROM CENTRE OF ROMAN LAY-OUT]

B. FLEAM DYKE, CAMBS.

SECTION THROUGH
SCARP OF VALLUM
75 YARDS SOUTH-EAST
OF RAILWAY CUTTING

SCARP [SOUTH]

IRON SLAG
HORN CORE OF OX
POTSHERD [SOFT PASTE]
LIMIT OF EXCAVATION

ARTIFICIAL DEPOSITS
EXPLANATION OF SYMBOLS:
HUMUS
DIRTY CHALK RUBBLE
CLEAN WHITE CHALK RUBBLE
DISINTEGRATED CHALK

NATURAL DEPOSITS
OLD SURFACE SOIL OVERLYING CHALK ROCK

GROUND LEVEL

POTSHERD (SOFT PASTE)
CHARCOAL
POTSHERD (SOFT PASTE)
CUT BONE
FRAGMENT SAMIAN WARE
LUMPS OF IRON SLAG
POTSHERD (HARD)
SAMIAN? (SOFT PASTE)
FRAGMENT SAMIAN
POTSHERD (GRITTED WARE)

SCALE OF FEET:

EXPLANATION OF SYMBOLS EMPLOYED IN SECTION A

A = GRAVEL
B = CHALK RUBBLE
C = EARTH [TURF?]
D = PUDDLED CHALK
E = EARTH (PARTLY SURFACE SOIL)
F = CHALK ROCK

See pp. 129-31.

PLATE XIX

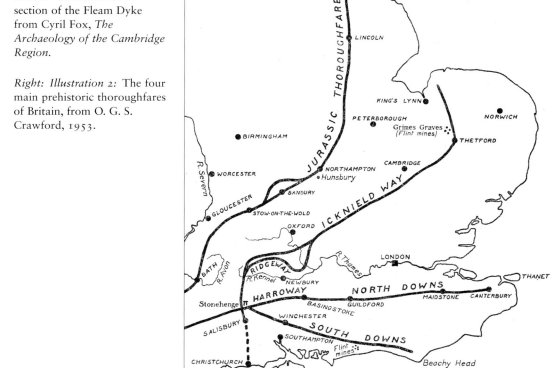

Above: Illustration 1: A section of the Fleam Dyke from Cyril Fox, *The Archaeology of the Cambridge Region.*

Right: Illustration 2: The four main prehistoric thoroughfares of Britain, from O. G. S. Crawford, 1953.

LINCOLN

JURASSIC THOROUGHFARE

KING'S LYNN
NORWICH
PETERBOROUGH
Grimes Graves (Flint mines)
THETFORD

BIRMINGHAM

CAMBRIDGE
NORTHAMPTON
Hunsbury
ICKNIELD WAY

R. Severn
WORCESTER

BANBURY
GLOUCESTER
STOW-ON-THE-WOLD
OXFORD

R. Thames
LONDON

BATH
R. Avon
RIDGEWAY
R. Kennet
NEWBURY
THANET
HARROWAY
NORTH DOWNS
Stonehenge
BASINGSTOKE
GUILDFORD
MAIDSTONE
CANTERBURY
WINCHESTER
SALISBURY
SOUTHAMPTON
Flint mines
SOUTH DOWNS
CHRISTCHURCH
Beachy Head

0   20   40   60   80 miles

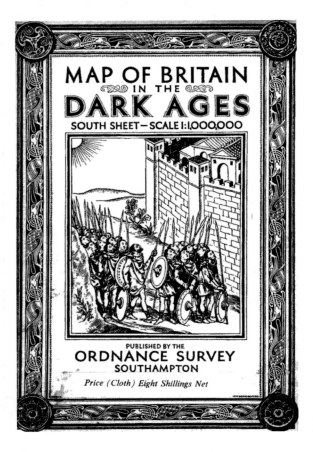

Illustration 3: Cover of the Ordnance Survey Map of Britain, the Dark Ages.

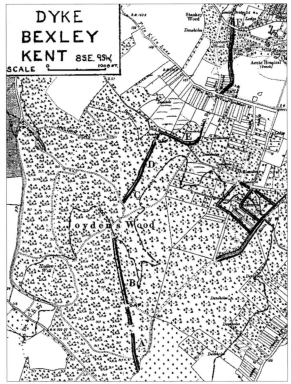

Illustration 4: The *Faesten Dic* from H. A. Hogg, 'Earthworks in Joydens Wood, Bexley, Kent'.

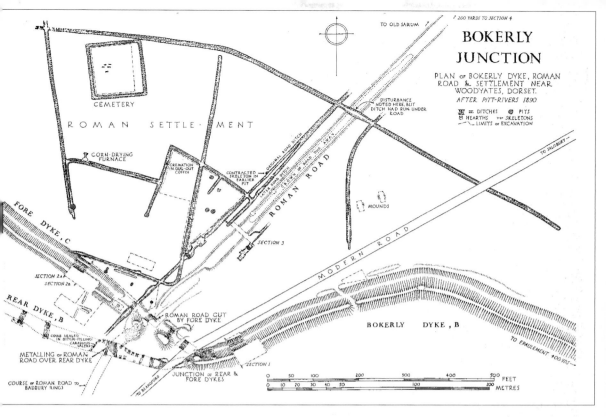

Illustration 5: Detail of Bokerly Dyke at Bokerly Junction after Pitt Rivers.

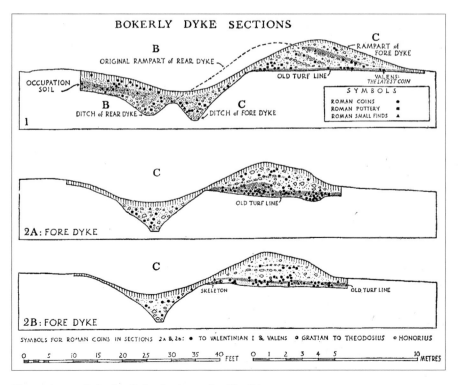

Illustration 6: Bokerley Dyke Sections after Pitt Rivers.

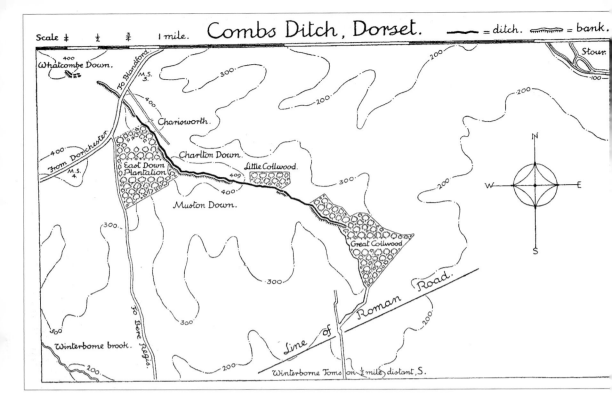

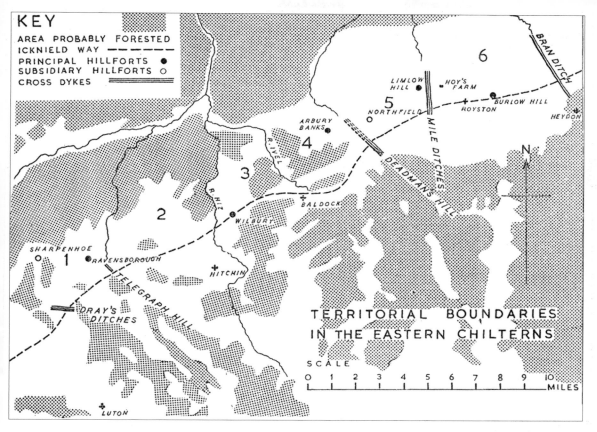

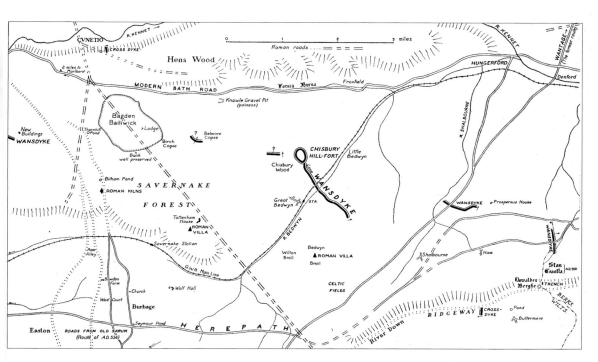

Illustration 9: Suggested boundaries in the Chilterns, from J. Dyer, 1963.

Illustration 10: The 'East Wansdyke' from O. G. S .Crawford, 1953. The dykes around Chisbury Hillfort are no longer regarded as part of the Wansdyke.

Above: Photo 1: Bokerley Dyke snakes through the countryside on the Wiltshire and Dorset border. (*Author*)

Left: Photo 2: The Wansdyke in Wiltshire showing the scale of the dyke. (*Courtesy of Wiltshire Council Archaeology Service*)

Photo 3: Conservation work on the Devil's Dyke, Cambridgeshire. The dykes are vulnerable to erosion. (*Author*)

Photo 4: The Devil's Dyke in Cambridgeshire is very stable due to the angle of the bank. (*Author*)

Above: Photo 5: Another view of the Devil's Dyke in Cambridgeshire, here cut by a railway line. (*Author*)

Left: Photo 6: The Roman Rig in woods near Greasbrough, which may be post-Roman in date. (*Author*)

Photo 7: Another view of the Roman Rig showing how vulnerable dykes can be to damage. (*Author*)

Photo 8: Here the Roman Rig only survives in the name of the Lane. (*Author*)

Above: Photo 9: An aerial view of Offa's Dyke at Llanfair Hill Shropshire; the white dots are sheep, showing the scale of the dyke. (*Courtesy of Clwyd Powys Archaeological Trust*)

Left: Photo 10: East of Montgomery Offa's Dyke cuts a straight line through the landscape. (*Courtesy of the Clwyd Powys Archaeological Trust*)

Photo 11: East of Treuddyn Offa's Dyke survives as the wooded bank above the road. (*Courtesy of the Clwyd Powys Archaeological Trust*)

Photo 12: This scheduled section of Offa's Dyke is south-west of Whitford and may not be part of the main dyke at all. (*Courtesy of the Clwyd Powys Archaeological Trust*)

Photo 13: A view of Wat's Dyke south-west of Northop, Flintshire. (*Courtesy of the Clwyd Powys Archaeological Trust*)

Photo 14: The Lower Short Ditch, Clun, Shropshire is one of the 'Short Dykes'. It can be seen in the woods to the bottom of the photograph. (*Courtesy of the Clwyd Powys Archaeological Trust*)

By the 80s AD the Roman army was campaigning in Scotland. Here a line of forts, watchtowers and fortlets was constructed, on the Roman road alongside the Gask ridge in Perthshire. Though not a continuous line of defence it was the earliest fortified frontier in Britain and possibly in the entire Roman Empire.

The Romans reorganised the social structure of Britain, by dividing up tribes and taking land to create their own communities. Roman Britain had a hierarchy of communities. At the top were the *Coloniae*, communities of Roman citizens, originally established as settlements for retired legionaries. Colchester (Camulodunum), Gloucester (Glevum) and Lincoln (Lindum) were all Colonia. London and York were not founded as Colonia but promoted to that status sometime in the Roman period. Each Colonia had a *territorium* of land around it that it administered. St Albans (Verulamium) was probably a *municipium*, a lower status than a colonia but where the inhabitants were still Roman citizens; a *municipium* also controlled a *territorium*. Lower still were the *civitaes perigrinae*, this designation covered the whole of a tribal territory and the area was administered from a civitas capital. It has often been claimed that the post-Roman dykes were used to mark the boundaries of a civitas (Laycock) or a colonia (R. E. Wheeler). Unfortunately we cannot be sure of the exact boundary of any Roman administration unit and the use of dykes to mark such boundaries can only be speculation.

By the second century the Roman Empire's political expansion had mostly ceased and frontiers were stabilised. The borders began to be fortified and made permanent. These defined and fortified frontiers were known as the *limes*. The actual line of the frontiers fluctuated as various emperors tried to expand the empire or gave up land to create more defensible frontiers.

In Germany the Roman frontier ran roughly along the line of the Rhine and Danube. To protect the area between the rivers successive emperors pushed the frontier forward here and fortified each frontier line. Hadrian built a palisade between the Rhine and Danube. Then Hadrian or possibly Antonius Pius pushed the frontier forward and built the *Pfahlgraben*, a bank with wooden stakes on top, fronted by a ditch. Where the *Pfahlgraben* ended the *Teufelsmauer* began, a straight wall for 50 km ending on the Danube near Regensburg. Like the British dykes, legends about the *limes* grew up. The *Teufelsmauer* was referred to as the Devil's Wall in the Middle Ages and there is a legend of a giant boar grubbing up the earth to form the *Pfahlgraben*.

From references in authors such as Tacitus, it seems the purpose of the Roman frontiers in Germany was as a line of control as much as a border defence. The control of trade in both directions across the frontier was made easier as traders were only allowed to use certain routes. It is not known if Hadrian's Wall operated a similar policy. Of all the post-Roman dykes in Britain, only the Wansdyke seems to have had gates built to control movement.

Around AD 122 Hadrian visited Britain, possibly to settle the northern frontier problem, and organised the construction of the stone wall that bears his name between the Solway and Tyne estuaries. His successor Antonius Pius abandoned Hadrian's Wall, pushed the frontier forward, and had a second wall constructed in turf on the Clyde to Forth line. This much shorter frontier line did not last and Antonius' successors pulled the frontier back to a refurbished Hadrian's Wall.

Hadrian's Wall is unusual in being built of stone, though this is not unique in the western Roman Empire, as the example of the *Teufelsmauer* described above shows. The traditional Roman material for linear defences was timber and turf, such as Caesar's temporary wall against the Helvetii.

The massive nature of the Hadrian' wall has even led to the suggestion that Hadrian may have been influenced by traveller's accounts of the Great Wall of China, built some 200 years before. (Breeze and Dobson). This is unlikely as at this time the wall built by the first Emperor of China (reigned 246–210 BC) had long been out of use. The series of walls now known as the Great Wall were not completed until the Ming period, at the end of the sixteenth century (Waldron). There were plenty of other models for Hadrian's Wall closer to home. J. G. Crow points out that there were a series of long walls in stone in the Eastern Mediterranean for Hadrian to draw on as models. Hadrian, who was a philhellene, may have imitated the Greek walls of the east instead of more traditional Roman military models. The first phase of Hadrian's Wall was originally built of turf, before being rebuilt in stone and the Antonine Wall was entirely turf built.

Greek walls in the east included the wall in the Thracian Chersonese built by Miltiades around 550 BC, and refortified in late Antiquity. There were also stone walls in the Crimea, such as the wall of Asander, 63 km long, to protect against steppe nomads. The walls of the Crimea and the Caucasian passes don't appear in the written records of later antiquity very much as they were far from the centre of power in Constantinople. For the Balkan long defences we have much have fuller information, such as the defences of the *Claustra Alpium Juliarum* in the Julian Alps and the passes in the Eastern Bulgaria of late Roman to Byzantine date. Four long walls are the most important in the written record: the walls on the Isthmus of Corinth; the defences of Thermopylae, both in Greece; the Long Walls of Chersonese near Gallipoli; and the Anastasian long walls of Thrace which protected Constantinople. The ancient defences across the Isthmus of Corinth were rebuilt *c.* AD 260 against the Goths and were used throughout the Byzantine period, lastly being repaired by Michael II Paleologus in AD 1415 by which time the enemy were the Ottoman Turks. Apart from the Thracian wall, all the walls were shorter than the 117 km of Hadrian's Wall and shorter than Aurelian's wall around Rome.

J. G. Crow also points out that the Roman frontier against Persia was not defined by walls; only a demarcation line was made. Long defensive walls were built to hold off barbarian invaders who did not have the resources for a long siege. The longer British dykes were unlikely to have been used in the same way as there is no evidence that they were manned along their length. Also there is no evidence of the associated structures to use a linear defences in this way such as the beacons and signal towers. If they were constructed of wood they would leave very little evidence but nothing has been found associated with a dyke. Also there is no evidence for the construction of roads behind the dykes to move troops around.

There is also a perception that in the late Roman Empire linear defences were no longer effective. However as Gildas understood, if properly manned a wall was effective against invaders. 'The British were told to construct across the island a wall linking the two seas: properly manned, this would scare away the enemy and act as a protection for the people.' (Gildas).

There is another factor in Britain that needs to be mentioned, the tradition of building earthwork defences around towns. Some Romano-British towns had walls built of earth, before being rebuilt in stone. This is unusual for the Roman world, it is not known in Gaul for example. The towns of Gaul had stone walls built in the late Roman period. Earth walls are not universal in Britain, some towns had them and others didn't. The dating of these earth walls is difficult, but around the period AD 190 has been suggested by Frere. It is difficult to link this wall building with a specific threat to Britain at this period. Earthwork walls are quick to build and can use unskilled labour but the gates were built of stone, suggesting that the threat was not urgent.

At the end of the Roman period Hadrian's Wall seems to have been abandoned around AD 400 (Esmonde Cleary). Only at the fort of Birdoswald is there evidence of post-Roman occupation with timber halls constructed over the remains of Roman granaries. The memory of when both of the walls were built seems to have vanished by Gildas' time, around AD 550. Gildas records that after the usurpation of Maximus Britain was despoiled of her military resources and threatened by the Scots and Picts. The Britons sent envoys to the Romans who dispatched a legion to drive away the invaders and then were told to construct a wall to link the two seas. 'But it was the work of a leaderless and irrational mob and made of turf rather than stone: so it did no good.' (Gildas)

After this the Scots and Picts returned. Following a second appeal to the Romans they returned and put the Scots and Picts to flight for a second time. Then 'they built a wall quite different from the first. This one ran from sea to sea, linking towns that happened to have been sited there out of fear of the enemy ...' (Gildas)

This wall was also abandoned by the Britons. Gildas here clearly has knowledge of the Antonine Wall and Hadrian's Wall and their different methods of construction but has no knowledge of when they were built.

The Anglo-Saxon Settlements

By the time of Augustine's arrival in Kent in AD 598 there were a number of Anglo-Saxon kingdoms. How these kingdoms formed has been the subject of academic debate. Attempts have been made to derive the boundaries of the Anglo-Saxon kingdoms from the remains of the British civitates (Dark, Laycock). In this model the new Anglo-Saxon rulers simply took over the existing political structure and boundaries of the civitas from their post-Roman rulers. However, this does not really convince, not least because there are uncertainties about of the boundaries of some of the British civitates. The other view is that early Anglo-Saxon kingdoms appear to have grown by the amalgamation of much smaller units (Bassett). The Anglo-Saxon Chronicle's view of the origins of the English kingdoms is not of much help as its information about the foundation of each kingdom seems suspiciously repetitive. The chronicle shows each kingdom as the creation of a heroic founding figure that lands at a specific place, battles against the Britons and founds a dynasty. However, the Anglo-Saxon Chronicle and Bede also incidentally record the existence of many smaller political units or sub-kingdoms. One such is the Jutish kingdom in Hampshire later absorbed by Wessex. There are also the areas that Bede refers to as 'regions' which once seem to have been independent political units, possibly under British control. Three of these areas in the north of England are Craven, Elmet and Hadfield. There is particular interest in Elmet as it was the British kingdom that seems to have survived for the longest time east of the Pennines. The Aberford Dykes were once suggested as forming the boundary of Elmet, as were the other Yorkshire dykes.

If the Anglo-Saxon kingdoms grew by absorbing smaller units then potentially boundaries would change rapidly. This makes relating the dykes to any possible early political boundaries extremely difficult.

The Germanic Background

> The construction of linear earthworks (such as the Cambridgeshire Dykes) in eastern Britain may also be evidence for this elite. These would necessitate a great amount of labour and, while this might have been a communal effort among peers, it is more likely the outcome of direction. The dykes represent another aspect of the fusion of British and Germanic culture – in 'free Germania' people did not construct such dykes but they did in fifth – and sixth-century western Britain.
>
> (Dark)

This quote is typical of the view that sees the culture of the post-Roman centuries entirely from the perspective of local Romano-British tradition and not from the Germanic culture of the Anglo-Saxons. Also it is a circular argument, the dykes in western Britain are assumed to belong to the fifth and sixth centuries and therefore be British. Developments are always seen as being of local British origin or being brought from western Britain. There are plenty of examples of linear earthworks across 'free Germania' that could possibly be the forerunners of the dykes in East Anglian and in other parts of Britain.

The earliest reference we have to a linear earthwork in 'free Germania' is from Tacitus' *Annals*. Tacitus describes a Roman army being ambushed in AD 16 at 'a narrow swampy open space enclosed between a river and the forest which in turn was surrounded by a deep morass (except on one side where a wide earthwork had been constructed by the Angrivrii to mark the Cheruscan frontier)' (Tacitus, *The Annals of Imperial Rome* 2, 19–20).

The Angrivarii and Cherusci were north German tribes whose territory was around the area of the middle Weser. In another of Tacitus' work, *The Histories*, he describes the political chaos following the deposition and suicide of the emperor Nero in AD 68. The following year AD 69 was known as the year of the four emperors as various claimants clashed for the imperial throne. The Germans took advantage of the confusion to attack neighbouring Gaulish tribes. During the chaos the Treveri built an earthwork as a protection. 'Moreover the Treveri had constructed a breastwork and rampart across their territory, and they and the Germans continued to contend with great losses on both sides up to the time when they tarnished by rebellion their distinguished services to the Roman people.' (Tacitus, *Complete Works of Tacitus*, 4, 37)

The Treveri were a tribe of eastern Gaul, who occupied the area of the lower Moselle valley and who were old allies of the Romans. They had been absorbed into the Roman Empire by about 30 BC. So by AD 69 it would have been about a century since the Treveri were independent from Rome.

Further to the east Ammianus Marcellinus records how in the fourth century AD the Goths, under pressure from the Huns and their allies the Alans, were pushed back east of the River Dniester. The response of the Gothic king Athanaricus was recorded by Ammianus Marcellinus.

> Athanaricus, troubled by this unexpected attack and still more through fear of what might come, had walls built high, skirting the lands of the Taifali from the banks of the river Gerasus as far as the Danube, thinking that by this hastily but diligently constructed barrier his security and safety would be assured. But while this well-planned work was being pushed on, the Huns swiftly fell upon him, and would have crushed him at once on their arrival had they not been so loaded down with booty that they gave up the attempt.
>
> (Marcellinus, Book 31, 3,1)

Attempts have been made to link this wall of Athanaric with earthworks in southern Moldavia. Peter Heather (Heather) has pointed out that these earthworks do not go anywhere near the land of the Taifali (modern Oltenia) and do not run to the Danube. Instead, Heather has suggested that the Goths reused the old Roman *limes transalutanus*, instead of constructing a new line of defences.

Denmark

Moving back to Western Europe there are several major linear earthworks in Denmark. In a famous passage Bede describes the origins of the English as coming from three tribes: the Angles, the Saxons and the Jutes.

> These new-comers were from the three most formidable races of Germany, the Saxons, Angles, and Jutes. From the Jutes are descended the people of Kent and the Isle of Wight and those in

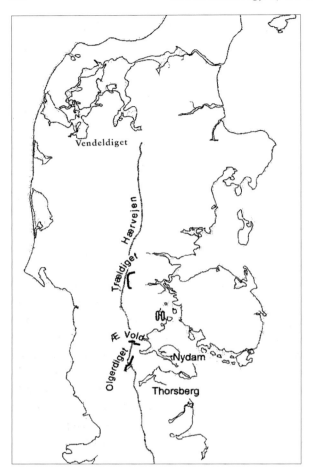

Map 29: Dykes in Denmark.

the province of the West Saxons opposite the Isle Wight who are called Jutes to this day. From the Saxons – that is, the country now known as the land of the Old Saxons came the East, South and West Saxons. And from the Angle – that is, the country known as Angulus, which lies between the provinces of the Jutes and Saxons and is said to remain unpopulated to this day – are descended the East and Middle Angles, the Mercians, all the Northumbrian stock (that is, those peoples living north of the river Humber), and the other English peoples.

(Bede 1.15)

The area Bede called *Angulus* is also known as Angeln and lies at the base of the Jutland peninsula, straddling the modern border between Denmark and Germany, while the Jutes occupied the northern part of the peninsula, now called Jutland. Up the centre of the Jutland peninsula runs the Hærvejen or the royal road. While the road is ancient, the name Hærvejen is a modern one only used from the 1930s; it is a Danicised form of the German 'Heerweg' or military road. The Hærvejen was previously known by several names including the Cattle Road, the Oxen Road, the King's Road and the Main Road. This shows its main purpose was made to move cattle down towards the markets in the cities of north Germany and occasionally be used for the transport of troops. It was also a major pilgrimage route in medieval times. The Hærvejen was not a single road but a collection of tracks and sunken roads, running along the watershed of Jutland, between the rivers that flow east to the Baltic and those that flow west to the North Sea. The road runs from Viborg in the north to Hamburg in Germany. The actual date of the Hærvejen is not known but the routes are associated with the '*Waffenopferfunde*' or 'weapon sacrifices' from this time (Andresen, Iversen & Jensen). The *Waffenopferfunde* are large deposits of weapons and equipment found in the Danish bogs. Often the weapons have been ritually broken or burnt before being cast into the bog. Interestingly the weapon sacrifices seem to be confined to the eastern side of the Jutland peninsula with the Hærvejen and the associated dykes forming a boundary for this practice.

The major linear earthworks in Denmark include the Olgerdiget, the Æ Vogt, the Trældediget and the Margrethediget, the Vendeldiget and Rammedige as well as several minor ones. Diget is Danish for dyke. Not all of them are related to the Hærvejen.

The Olgerdiget is the southernmost of these defensive works along the Hærvejen (Christensen). It consisted of three lines of palisades, a ditch and an embankment. The bank is now mostly flattened and only found in a few isolated places. The ditch was flat bottomed, about 1.6 m deep and 4 m wide and water filled. The palisades only survive as a line of post holes running parallel to the ditch. They seem to represent different phases of rebuild and repair as the stakes in the palisades are not uniform in cross section or in depth of post holes. The third line of the palisade is the youngest, and made from slightly smaller posts. The complex is about 12 km long in total but the palisade only runs for about 7½ km in front of the ditch. The excavators estimate that about 90,000 posts were needed to build the palisade. This is a substantial monument showing the ability of a group of people that was able to mobilise resources from much more than a local scale.

The original dendrochronological dates on wood from the post holes showed that Olgerdiget was built shortly after AD 219, and repeatedly repaired, the last line of palisades being built not later than AD 278. Around AD 300 Olgerdiget was abandoned. The dates were used to claim a link with the Roman *limes* in Germany as a direct model for the Olgerdiget. Recently new dates from the Olgerdiget showed that the monument was build after AD 40–50, phase two was around AD 70 and phase three around AD 90. Phase two are three are more closely dated because the wood samples had sapwood attached. I am grateful to Per Ethelberg from the Sønderjylland (South Jutland) Museum for this information. The Olgerdiget may have been the boundary between the Jutes and the Angles and Olgerdiget could have acted as a customs barrier as well as a possible tribal boundary.

The Æ Vold also known as the Vendersvold is now dated from around AD 150. The dyke was originally about 3 km long but only about 500 m survive today with the ditch lying to the north of the bank. The new dating shows that it is not contemporary with the Olgerdiget as once thought.

The Trældiget has attracted the attention of archaeologists from the time of Worsaae in 1841 onwards. Unfortunately there has been little excavation of this

10–15-kilometre-long dyke and interpretation was hampered by lack of evidence on issues such as the dyke's construction, extent and date. The first modern excavation was done in 1981 along the line of a natural gas pipe. The excavation confirmed that the Trældiget was a defensive work of very considerable dimensions with a moat, a bank and associated palisade. Further excavations in advance of new road building were done in 1994 (Knudsen and Rindel). When A. P. Madsen mapped the Trældiget in 1894 the bank stood more than 2.5 m high. Today most of the Trældiget has now been flattened by erosion, cultivation and road building.

The modern excavation has shown that the ditch was 2–3 m wide and 1.5–2 m deep. The ditch seems to have gone out of use and started filling up by the early middle ages. The 1994 excavation found there was an earlier phase of a small bank and ditch to the west of the later Trældiget. The later and still visible ditch had a Y-shaped cross section with a narrow slot at the base. The excavation also found a narrow trench in front of the ditch, which was interpreted as a slot for a palisade. Unfortunately the preliminary excavation report did not provide a firm date for the construction of the Trældiget, only that it overlay a settlement of the early Iron Age, approximately the first to third centuries BC, and a date in the Roman Iron Age is most probable.

Of the other dykes along the Hærvejen the Margrethediget survives as a 150-metre-long embankment at a right angle to the Hærvejen. The date of the Margrethediget is unknown as no excavation has taken place. The Vendeldiget means the winding dyke or curved dyke and is situated in western Jutland. It has now been ploughed flat and is visible only as a crop mark 3.75 km long. Excavations between 1992 and 1995 showed that the ditch varied in width from 2 to 3.3 m and varied in cross section from U-shape to V-shaped (Mikkelsen and Olesen). The excavators suggested it could be the work of four to five villages under the direction of a local chieftain.

The largest of the dykes, the Danevirke, was once in Denmark but now is in Germany. The Danevirke (also known as the Daneverk, Dannevirke or Danewerk), simply means the 'Dane's work'. It is the name for the Danish defensive wall which stretches from the moors of west Jutland to the town of Schleswig, situated at Slien at the Baltic Sea, near the Viking trade centre of Hedeby.

According to written sources (Nithard), the work on Danevirke was initiated by the Danish King Godofrid in AD 808.

But Godofrid before his return destroyed a trading place on the seashore, in Danish called Reric, which, because of the taxes it paid, was of great advantage to his kingdom. Transferring the merchants from Reric he weighed anchor and came with his whole army to the harbour of Schleswig. There he remained for a few days and decided to fortify the border of his kingdom against Saxony with a rampart, so that a protective bulwark would stretch from the eastern bay called Ostarsalt, as far as the western sea, along the entire north bank of the River Eider and broken by a single gate thorough which wagons and horsemen would be able to leave and enter. After dividing the work among the leaders of his troops he returned home.

(Nithard)

Reric is the modern town of Lübeck. Fearing an invasion by the Franks, Godofrid built an enormous structure for the defence of his realm, which separated the Jutland Peninsula from the northern part of the Frankish empire. However, archaeology has shown a slightly different picture. Excavation between 1969 and 1975 showed three building phases of the main structure of Danevirke. The phases were dendrochronologically dated between AD 737 and AD 968. Either Godofrid refurbished an existing structure or extended the earthwork so his name became attached to the whole monument. There are interesting parallels to Offa's Dyke here, which is of approximately the same date. Both monuments are described as stretching from sea to sea and are recorded as being the work of one king but archaeology has shown a more complicated picture, the monument being a development of several stages.

The first phase of the Danevirke consisted of three parts the Hovedvolden from the River Rheider Au (or Rejde Å) in Danish to the Dannevirke Sø lake. The second section is the Nordvolden running from the north-eastern side of Dannevirke Sø, for 7 km. This runs north of the town of Hedeby. The final part is the Østervolden which protects the Schwansen peninsula. Volden is Danish for rampart.

The second phase is an extension that stretched from Rheide Å for about 7 km to Schlei bay. This may be the extension recorded by the Frankish Royal Annals above. Significantly this southern extension protected the town of Hedeby. The final phase consists of a number of earthworks that extended the Danevirke and strengthened weak points of the system. These parts have names such as Hovedvolden (main rampart), Krumvolden (curved rampart); Buevolden (bow rampart); Dobbeltvolden (double rampart); Forbindelsesvolden (connecting rampart) and Margarethenwall (Margret's rampart).

The Danevirke has a total length of about 30 km total, and measures between 3.5 and 6 m in height. During the middle ages, the structure was enhanced with palisades and walls, and used by Danish kings as a gathering point for Danish military excursions and crusades, particularly the Danish raids against the Slavs. In the twelfth century, King Valdemar I reinforced parts of Danevirke with a brick wall, which underlines the continued strategic and military importance of the structure throughout the middle ages. Danevirke was last used as a means of Danish defence in the Danish-Prussian war of 1864, without much success however. It was badly maintained and during the war, Danevirke was quickly captured by the Austrians and Prussians, and following the Prussian occupation of Schleswig and Southern Jutland ('Slesvig' or 'Sønderjylland' in Danish), the Danevike became part of Prussia in a united Germany. During the Second World War the Germans integrated Danevirke into their defences against a feared allied invasion from the North Sea.

The other important dyke in Scandinavia is the Götavirke in southern Sweden. The Götavirke (Geatish Dyke) is a dyke running north to south between two villages called Västra Husby and Hylinge in Ostrogothia, southern Sweden. The dyke lies between lakes Asplången and Lillsjön. There have been suggestions that several hillforts north of Aspelången may have been part of the same defensive line. South of Lake Lillsjön, difficult terrain makes a defence line unnecessary. After excavation work in the 1930s by Arthur Nordén, he suggested that the Götavirke was built in the period between the early and late Iron Age around AD 500. However excavations in 1985 (Nielsen) to check on the condition of the monument found wood fragments that appeared to come from a palisade. Radiocarbon dating of these fragments suggested that the Götavirke was much earlier in date around the early Roman Iron age to late Roman Iron age. The excavators suggested that the Götavirke was contemporary with the Olgerdiget.

We cannot dismiss a Germanic origin of the English dykes out of hand. There is a long tradition of building linear earthworks in northern Europe. This tradition stretches from the early Iron Age through to the medieval period and is also concentrated in those areas we know Germanic migrants came from.

Dating the Dykes

When the dykes were built is crucial to understanding them and to decide who built them and if they are all contemporary monuments. As we have seen O. G. S. Crawford dated many of the dykes to the post-Roman period by comparison of their form with other monuments he believed were of similar date. This reliance on style led to circular arguments and the misdating of several sites. There seems no evidence to link the boundary of any particular post-Roman groups with a dyke.

Dating the dykes can be problematic. Dating evidence is scarce and most excavations of the dykes have produced no useful evidence that can be used for dating, or at best only ambiguous evidence. Also dykes built across open country will have little chance of material getting into banks or the filling of ditches. The most likely type of artefact is pottery which is durable so it likely to be lying around in the soil but this depends on local use of pottery. In the post-Roman period pottery went out of use for a long period. No dyke has been excavated completely, only small sections cut into them. For example the Roman Ridge has had at least five excavations since the 1940s and the total number of artefacts found is zero.

It must be remembered that any artefacts can only give a *Terminus post quem (TPQ)* or date after which a feature was built. Roman pottery in the fill of a ditch shows the ditch began to fill up in the Roman period or after but not how long after. Depending on factors such as maintenance, soil and ground cover, ditches may take centuries to fill up. In the case of the Aberford Dykes, excavations showed second-century AD Roman pottery in the filling of the ditch of Becca Banks, while radiocarbon dates from animal bone in the same layer gave much later dates so the pottery was residual. Artefacts sealed by the bank of a dyke give a clearer picture.

Scientific dating techniques hold promise for getting better dates for the dykes but may not be precise enough to show if a dyke was built in AD 450 or AD 600. As we have seen a recent campaign of excavation and radiocarbon dating has resolved the date of some of the Welsh Short Dykes.

There are two scientific dating techniques that have only recently been applied the dykes; optically stimulated luminescence dating (OSL) and archaeomagnetic dating.

Both these techniques have been applied to the dating of the Scot's Dyke and have shown it is Iron Age, not post-Roman. Both techniques have been used to date the deposition of the sediment in the ditch directly, not to date artefacts. This should prevent the problem of residual material giving a date that is too early.

Unfortunately one of the most precise techniques available, dendrochronology, can only be useful in the rare circumstances where wet conditions allow wood to survive. It is unlikely to be useful to date any of the English dykes, though by chance wood was found at the Dorsey in Northern Ireland (Baillie & Brown) and was able to be dated. Excavation also found dateable wood at the Olgerdiget in Denmark.

One of the arguments put forward for the building of the dykes by the Romano-British in the period before the arrival of the Anglo-Saxons is the frequency of the name Grim's Ditch or Grim's Dyke and also Devil's Dyke or Devil's Ditch. This comes from the old English *Grim* meaning the old one, a nickname for the pagan god Woden. The suggestion is the Anglo-Saxons did not know who built the dykes so they attributed them to Woden. Later on when Christianity arrived Woden was equated with the devil and some names were changed to the Devil's Dyke or Ditch.

The problem with this argument is that only one of the Grim's Dykes/Ditches can be shown definitely to be post-Roman, the monument in Pear Wood Pinner. The West Yorkshire Grim's Ditch is Iron Age and so is the 'Chiltern Grim's Ditch'. Also the Berkshire ditches, part of the 'Silchester Dykes', are likely to be prehistoric. We do not know when the name Grim's Dyke or Devil's Dyke was first applied to any of the dykes. In the medieval chronicle of John of Fordun, the Antonine wall is called the Gryme's Dyke. The names seem to be used indiscriminately and interchangeably by antiquarians.

The Devil's Dyke in Cambridgeshire must be a post-medieval name, as in medieval documents both the Devil's Dyke and the Fleam Ditch are referred to as simply '*the dic*' or the great ditch. The Devil's Dyke was also known as St Edmund's Dyke as it marked the limit of the diocese of Bury St Edmunds.

The Wansdyke, east and west, is the only monument named after Woden directly and it may have been attributed to Woden because the Anglo-Saxons did not know who built it. There is an alternative explanation through three other Woden names that exist in relation to the East Wansdyke: *Wodnes beorge*, 'Woden's Hill', a Neolithic long barrow now called Adam's Grave; *Wodnes dene*, a valley; and *Woddes geat*, a battle site somewhere in Berkshire. Possibly a sanctuary or temple to Woden was built by the Anglo-Saxons to mark the building of the East Wansdyke and this name was transferred to the earthwork itself.

Faestendic, the 'strong dyke' is also a common name for dykes. Examples exist for Kent and Surrey, the dyke on Hartford Bridge Flats and in Hampshire for the Devil's Ditch near Andover. As well as part of the Chiltern Grim's Ditch; the Great Missenden to Wendover section was described as '*Fastendich*' in Missenden Abbey documents. The Chiltern Grim's Ditch and the Devil's Ditch Andover are prehistoric and the other three are of possible post-Roman date but not certain. This appears to be a name given to any larger or stronger dyke in the area. In Wales there are similar descriptive names, there are two dykes called Clywdd Mawr, Welsh for Big Ditch.

CHAPTER 4
THE FUNCTION OF THE DYKES

Having examined the archaeology of the dykes it is now time to look at their function. The definite post-Roman dykes are widely separated, with a concentration in East Anglia, with examples in Middlesex, Dorset and Derbyshire and another major concentration along the Welsh border. There are possible examples in Kent, Surrey and Hampshire.

Most authors have assumed the dykes were built as defences or as boundary markers though another suggestion is that the dykes were ritual in function:

> They were apparently constructed in the fifth and sixth centuries, and may have had a ritual dimension, terminating at Roman-period temples and springs or wet areas associated with deposited weapons. A protective purpose seems to be their primary function, and ritual may be one aspect of this as perceived by their designers.
>
> (Dark)

There is no evidence of any of the dykes having a primary ritual function. There have never been any deposits of a ritual nature found near the dykes. Of course monuments have a symbolic status as well as a practical purpose but it is unlikely that any of the dykes were built purely for a ritual purpose.

There are some problems with the dykes as purely defensive monuments. The dykes can be divided in two groups based on their size. The 'long dykes' such as Offa's Dyke, Wat's Dyke, the Devil's Dyke in Cambridgeshire and possibly the other Cambridgeshire Dykes form one group. They need a large amount of manpower and organisation to build and need to draw on more than the local area for resources. The second group are the shorter dykes which seem to block or control movement along Roman roads. Grim's Ditch Pear Wood, Grey Ditch and Bokerley Dyke are examples of the shorter dykes. They would be easier to build than the bigger dykes only needing local manpower. Both types of dykes are uncertain at their ends, and seem to end 'in air'. The theory that ends were blocked by forest is no longer tenable, though marsh may form the ends of the Cambridgeshire Dykes.

The shorter dykes do not seem to be designed to stop a large invasion force because a determined attacker could go round the dyke. They are more likely designed to stop small parties of raiders, or to control and to tax movement of people or goods by forcing them to use designated routes.

The longer dykes are much grander monuments and run across the country but again as defensive monuments they have problems. There is no evidence of watch towers or signal stations as found on Hadrian's Wall or any associated roads for the movement of troops. It is highly unlikely that the full length of any of the dykes could have been manned for any length of time. All any enemy had to do was to concentrate enough troops against one part of the dyke to overwhelm the defenders. If the defenders drew in more of their own forces to meet this threat they left other areas vulnerable to attack. Hadrian's Wall was only part of a much larger Roman defence system supported in depth by a large number of troops in forts behind the Wall.

One of the other ways that the dykes could have been used is as an agreed or negotiated boundary line between two groups. One historical example from a much later period is the earthwork known as the Old Scots Dike in Cumbria and the Scottish Borders. The Scots Dike was agreed upon as the boundary between England and Scotland through the area known as the debatable land in AD 1552. The border line was agreed by commissioners appointed by Mary Queen of Scots and Edward VI of England. The commissioners met and 'agreed on a line to be marked by a ditch and march stones' (Mack). The line runs from the River Esk to the River Sark and was marked with stones at each end carved with the arms of England and Scotland. Fortunately Mack was able to write about and describe the Scots Dike just before a large part of it was destroyed by forestry work in 1918 and 1919. Mack shows that the Scots Dike was not uniform in construction. Work was done by a number of gangs who each constructed a section. The dyke was built by digging two parallel trenches and heaping the spoil into the centre. There was not much coordination between the work gangs. At one place there is a gap of 6.5 m where two sections of dyke do not meet up. In other places there are two separate dykes about 9 m apart.

In a charter dating from between AD 672–674 a Mercian sub-king called Frithuwold granted land to Erkenwald who later became bishop of London, for his minster at Chertsey:

And the land is, taken together, 300 hides... the whole along the bank of the river as far as the boundary which is called the ancient ditch, that is Fullingadic ...

(Blair, 'Frithuwold's Kingdom and the origin of Surrey')

Fullingadic marks the boundary between the hundreds of Woking and Godalming and the Wealden districts on the east. This boundary was old by AD 670 when the Chertsey charter was drawn up.

A road runs south from the Thames at Weybridge to mark the parish boundary between Byfleet and Walton-on-Thames part of which is also marked by ditches on St George's Hill. John Blair suggests that this was the line of the *Fullingadic*, which may once have defined the area of the *Fullingas* – Fulla's people. The name Fulla may also appear as part of Fulham. If this is the same Fulla it would show a people or a leader in control of an area from west London to Surrey.

Surrey was the '*suðre ge*' the southern province. Blair strongly suggests that Surrey was part of an artificial Mercian province created by King Wulfhere for the sub-king Frithuwold. The *Fullingadic* is an obsolete boundary only recorded by chance because it was used as boundary marker for the Chertsey bequest. Other boundary dykes may have existed but were not documented.

There are two other boundary ditches in Surrey that may shed some light on this. A large ditch runs from the Thames to Surbiton Golf Club in a straight north–south direction, for a distance of some 4 km and forms the Thames Ditton and Long Ditton parish boundary. It has been suggested that it is possibly prehistoric or Roman construction and used to mark the parish boundary. A boundary bank also marks the Esher and Cobham parish boundary and the Surrey Historic Environmental Record suggests this is another Anglo-Saxon boundary.

Whether these Surrey dykes were built by the Anglo-Saxons or they just reused existing dykes as boundaries is unknown. This does show how dykes were used as boundary markers in the later Anglo-Saxon period where there was no existing feature to mark a boundary. The Iron Age Aves Ditch in Oxfordshire is another case of a reused prehistoric boundary.

Some of the Welsh Sort Dykes may also fit into this category of boundary markers. Stuart Laycock in *Britannia the Failed State* (2008) has suggested that Britain was marked by tribal conflicts throughout the period of Roman occupation and at the end of the Roman period tribal conflicts helped to create a failed state on the model of Yugoslavia or Somalia. The artificial civitas boundaries created by the Romans did not always match the tribal boundaries and were a source of tension. In Laycock's model the dykes play a central part. They are of very late Roman or early post-Roman date and are built to mark tribal boundaries. For Laycock the Wansdyke is a single monument, joined by the Roman road and marking the division between the Durotriges and the Dobunni.

> The much stronger tradition of linear earthwork defences in Britain as opposed to the continental homelands of the Anglo-Saxons, the inclusion of hillforts into the design, and the naming by the Anglo-Saxons of the dyke after a non-human figure Woden, rather than a person (common with pre-Anglo-Saxon earthworks, whether of a pre-Roman or post-Roman origin and implying they did not know its real origins) all suggest that Wansdyke is likely to be of British origin.
>
> (Laycock)

Similarly the Bokerley Dyke was built to protect the Durotriges from the Atrebates. The Icenian and Catuvellaunian border was marked first by the Iron Age Miles Ditches, which was replaced in the post-Roman period by the Fleam Ditch which marks the same frontier in a slightly different place.

The two sets of opposing dykes in Norfolk; The Beecham Ditch (*sic*) and Foss Ditch protect the Fens and the Lauditch and Panworth Ditch protect Icenian territory.

I won't discuss the problems of Laycock's model in details except to note he derives the boundaries of every Anglo-Saxon kingdom from the pre-existing Roman civitas boundaries. An exception is made for the Catuvellauni who break up into the smaller territories recorded in the later Anglo-Saxon document known as the *Tribal Hidage*. This is highly problematic, as we do not know the real Iron Age tribal boundaries or the Roman civitas that followed them. It also ignores some of the smaller territories we know about from Anglo-Saxon sources.

Laycock's model fails to account for a number of dykes not on the boundaries of civitates, such as the Grey Ditch in Derbyshire and the Comb's Ditch in Dorset. The claim that because the Wansdyke includes hillforts as part of its construction it is likely to be British is not a strong argument. The connection between the hillforts and the Wansdyke could be fortuitous. If the hillforts which were on the top of hills were used as sighting guides for the construction of the Wansdyke then the Wansdyke would naturally run close to a number of hillforts. The hillforts of Maes Knoll and Stantonbury on the Wansdyke don't seem to have any post-Roman occupation unlike other hillforts in Somerset at South Cadbury and Cadbury Congresbury. Offa's Dyke also incorporates hillforts in its construction for example at Castle Ring and Burfa Camp and so does Wat's Dyke at Old Oswestry.

An assumption has always been made that the ditch lay on the 'outside' of the dyke facing the direction of the threat but Wileman has pointed out that in common law the support for a fence should lie on the side of the builder. If the ditch is considered the quarry for the bank then it may lay on the 'inside' of the dyke. There is no evidence to support this theory. Offa's dyke mostly has a west-facing ditch. Also the gates on the Wansdyke if they are original show the ditch to be on the outside. All of the certain post-Roman dykes face westwards or northwards inland, suggesting strongly that they are Anglo-Saxon.

A distinction can be drawn between a frontier and a border. A frontier can be thought of as a zone while a border is a more or less defined line. It is possible that the real borders lay in front of the line of the dyke; in the case of the West Wansdyke it is possible that the Avon formed the frontier and the Wansdyke was a full back position. Alternatively there could be a zone in front of the dyke that was of uncertain status or agreed as a separation zone like the DMZ, the demilitarized zone between North and South Korea, ironically one of the most heavily fortified places on earth. There is also evidence from Wat's Dyke which lay further back, on lower ground, unlike Offa's Dyke. Was the area between Wat's Dyke and Offa's Dyke given up or was there a zone in front of Wat's Dyke that could be abandoned when danger threatened and people could move back into the safety of Wat's Dyke? The east Wansdyke has evidence of gates, if they are original to the monument, which suggests it was not constructed in a hurry. This again suggests a frontier zone used for pasture from which people could retreat if threatened. The zone beyond the Wansdyke could be used for seasonal pasturing of cattle or sheep.

There are a number of scenarios for dykes building. One case is where a strong group is threatened by a weaker group and imposes a boundary. Here the dyke builders must face a threat from a diffuse group and could not destroy or drive off the weaker group. The threat must be in the form of some kind of asymmetric warfare such as small scale raiding. Another scenario is where groups of roughly equal strength want to set a defined border in an uncertain area. An example is the building of the Scot's Dike between England and Scotland in the sixteenth century. A final and more unlikely scenario is where a weaker group want to protect themselves from a stronger group. This is not very likely. The stronger group may be provoked into pre-emptive action before the defences are complete. Also would a weak group mobilise enough resources to build a defensive earthwork?

There may be situations where there is a combination of an imposed boundary and a negotiated boundary at local level. This may explain some of the kinks and zigzags in the Wansdyke and Offa's Dyke.

A dyke may also be offensive rather than defensive, designed to cut off routes used by an enemy or to deny access to land. Bokerley Dyke and Wansdyke do block Roman roads that are never used again. It is difficult to tell if this is this cause or effect. Did the blocking of the road force traffic away or did the threat mean the only traffic on the road was hostile and so had to be blocked?

This book can be seen as a preliminary report on the dykes. Much work still needs to be done. Are the gaps seen in the dykes real? What happens at the end of the dykes? Dates need to be obtained for a lot more of the dykes using the latest scientific techniques to date the dyke materials directly. Only after two centuries of research and excavation are we getting to grips with the dykes. In the near future we may be able to answer the question when were the dykes built with better precision than ever. This may not give us the answer to the question why they were built. The dykes may retain some of their mystery.

APPENDIX 1

STRANGE IDEAS AND NON-EXISTENT DYKES

The dykes have always been the focus of some strange ideas. A Major P. Godsal wrote a pamphlet in 1913 to explain that the dykes must have been built to divide Saxons and Celts as peoples of the same race did not build such monuments. In 1905 Edward Wooler in his paper on the 'Catrail' joins the dots in a big way. The paper which is the 'result of three-and-a-half years of careful investigation' aims to show as its full title suggests 'The Catrail otherwise known as the "Black Dyke", "Scots Nick", and "Scots Dyke", all one and the same'. Wooler conflates several monuments: the Catrail in the Scottish Borders, the Black Dyke in Northumberland and the North Yorkshire Scots Dyke. This super monument ran for about 193 km between Galashiels and Richmond, with a suspiciously straight line on his map from Peel Fell to Allenheads. Wooler described it as a military work designed to protect against the Roman invasion. Wooler only managed to take his monument as far as Richmond but it seems he was tempted to join it to the Roman Ridge:

> This point is as far as I have carried out my investigations, though I hear of other entrenchments in the neighbourhood, which tend to confirm Warburton's theory that the dyke ran as far south as Wincobank, near Sheffield.

J. L. Ferns in 'Three Big Errors in History Books' claims that Offa's Dyke, Wat's Dyke and the Wansdyke were prehistoric trackways or roads, used to trade flint. On Offa's Dyke, 'The defence line idea can be ruled out straightaway because it was unnecessary, impractical and completely beyond the power of the tiny kingdom of Mercia to man it continuously.' Ferns claims that the dykes were not built deliberately by digging a ditch and making a bank but made by the feet of men and animals over a long period of time. In fact these are very old ideas going back to the first antiquarians where dykes were confused with trackways and vice-versa.

There are still modern references to a Dark Age dyke all the way around the borders of Galloway (Grigg), referring to the Deil's Dyke. The idea of such a dyke all around Galloway originates with an early nineteenth-century antiquarian called Joseph Train.

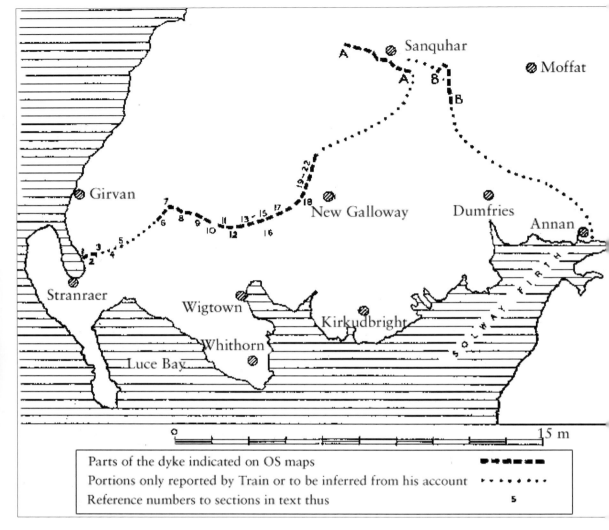

Map 30: The Deil's Dyke in Galloway after Graham.

Train (1779–1852) was the subject of a profile by Charles Dickens who wrote about the 'the worthy old antiquary' in *Household Words* in 1853, the year after his death.

> His antiquarian deeds were numerous and important, he traced an ancient wall, built, it is thought, by the aborigines, from Loch-ryan, in Wigtonshire, to the northeast border of the Stewartry of Kircudbright, where it joins Nithsdale. This wall the country people call the Deil's Dyke; it consists of a strong wall eight feet broad, the base of which is built of stones, or where stones were not to be had, of earth. Its course extends to more than fifty-three miles.
>
> (Dickens)

Train believed the dyke was post-Roman as did subsequent antiquarians. One such as G. V. Irving (Irving) who suggested in 1862 that the dyke must belong to the post-Roman period as Celtic tribes differed little in their level of civilisation, while the dyke was obviously built by the inhabitants of a settled district to keep out the uncivilised neighbours. When the Ordnance Survey marked the Deil's Dyke on their maps during their surveys between 1846 and 1850, it is possible they were influenced by Train's description of the dyke. Even the RCAHMS' inventories of Wigtownshire, Kirkcudbrightshire and Dumfriesshire 'assumed the existence of the dyke, treated its reputed remains more or less in isolation, and abstained, from a critical discussion of the whole' (Graham, *The Deil's Dyke in Galloway*).

It was not until Angus Graham re-examined the Deil's Dyke in the 1940s as a comparison with the Catrail that Train's theory of a continuous dyke from Loch Ryan across Galloway to the Solway coast collapsed. Train's dyke was simply not there, it was selected parts of agricultural dykes built as eighteenth-century land improvements, and in one place the hollow trackway of an old road was confused with the ditch of the dyke. The mix of drystone walls and earth banks also did not suggest the uniform construction of single phase linear earthwork. Also the gaps between sections were too large to explain by robbing of the stonework.

In a second paper in 1956 (Graham & Feachem, 'The Deil's Dyke in Dumfriesshire and Ayrshire'), Graham followed up with the description of the Deil's Dyke or Celtic Dyke in Nithsdale. This had been joined on to Train's great dyke, but Graham showed that while it was not as long as the Ordnance Survey had shown on the maps, it was a substantial dyke and a uniform earthwork. Also he makes a convincing case that the name could derive from the old Scots word *deil*, a part or portion or dale/daill which means a portion of land. The original name of the dyke would have been the Deil Dyke, not the Deil's or Devil's Dyke, which came later influenced by the similarity in sound to the English Devil's Dykes.

The remaining problem is the date of the dyke. Graham rejected the idea of an eighteenth-century dyke built for agricultural improvement due the length of the monument. A medieval date was also rejected because the Deil's Dyke did not fit to any known feudal boundaries. This left a strong suggestion of a Dark Age date. Unfortunately subsequent excavations have not resolved the dating of the dyke. Excavation in advance of destruction by the National Coal Board (Halpin) found that 80 per cent of the dyke in the threatened area had already been destroyed by agricultural practices since the 1950s. No dating evidence was found for the dyke.

THE CHILTERN GRIM'S DITCH

The Chilterns are a high ridge of chalk running north-east from the Thames in Oxfordshire, through Buckinghamshire, Hertfordshire and Bedfordshire. The geology is a soft chalk, sandwiched between Gault clay to the north and clay with flints to the south. There are a number of dykes along the Chiltern ridge. In a paper in *Antiquity* in 1931 (O. G. Crawford, 'The Chiltern Grim's Ditches') O. G. S. Crawford defined the dykes along the southern part of the ridge in Buckinghamshire and Hertfordshire as a single system. The Chiltern Grim's Ditch was made up of a number of individual dykes, all separately named the Grim's Ditch. The system also extended across the Thames into Berkshire and Oxfordshire. Crawford listed the three dykes making up the whole Grim's Ditch, from south to north, as:

The Aldworth Grims Ditch, later this was considered to be part of the Silchester dyke system by O'Neil in 'The Silchester Region in the 5th & 6th centuries AD' (see the section above on the Silchester Dykes).

The second part was the Mongwell or South Oxfordshire Grim's Ditch (see the entry on this earthwork under Oxfordshire in the Gazetteer).

The final part of the system was the Buckinghamshire and Hertfordshire Grim's Ditch which Crawford considered to be originally a single monument now split into four sections: Hampden; a section from Missenden to Lee; King's Ash to west of Berkhamsted and Berkhamsted Common. Though Crawford admitted, 'There is no evidence one way or another … it is highly probable that the now disparate sections all belonged to a single system.' Also Crawford notes that in a least one section, 'Here the Grim's Ditch commits tactical suicide, by deliberately leaving a steep slope and descending obliquely to the bottom of a valley.'

In Crawford's view the ditch was for defence against movement along the higher ground. As the ditches are on the northern side of these dykes it was assumed that the threat came from the north.

In a paper in a later issue of *Antiquity* titled 'Grimsditch and Cuthwulf's Expedition to the Chilterns in AD 57', Michael Hughes also assumes that the monument is a single work: 'I propose to assume, as I think I safely may, that the earthwork which

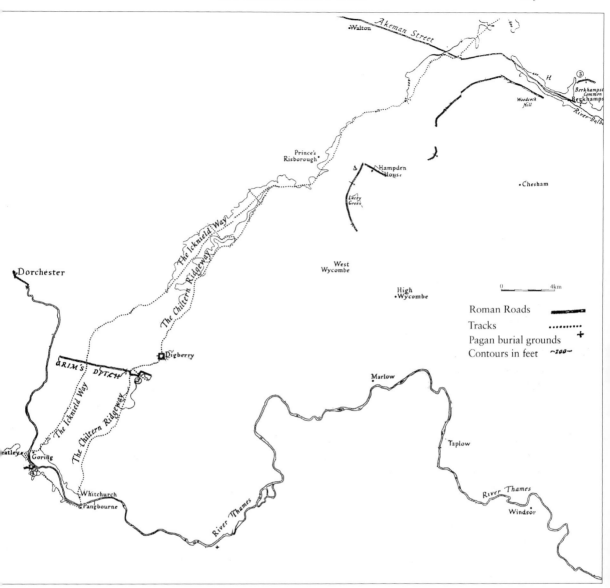

Map 31: The Grim's Ditches in the Chilterns.

runs from Berkhamsted to West Wycombe is a homogeneous whole'. Hughes then goes further and links the whole monument with the Saxon leader Cuthwulf. The Anglo-Saxon Chronicle records that in AD 571 Cuthwulf fought against the Britons at Bedcanford and captured four villages: Limbury, Aylesbury, Benson, and Eynsham. Hughes takes this entry as fact and uses it to deduce the Grimsditch (his spelling) was the northern boundary of Cuthwulf's conquests in AD 571. The Grim's Ditch was thus built as a boundary marker to protect the limits of the conquest of the Chilterns.

R. E. M. Wheeler and the Survival of Roman London

Sir Mortimer Wheeler used the Chiltern Grim's Ditch as part of his theory of the survival of London as a functioning community in the post-Roman period. He considered the Chiltern Grim's Ditch as a part of a system of defences around London, constructed to protect the capital from Anglo-Saxon invaders. In his 1934 paper in the *Antiquaries Journal*, Wheeler links the ancient right of Londoners to hunt in an area consisting of 'Middlesex, Hertfordshire and all Chiltern and all Kent as far as the Cray', which was granted by Henry I with the *territorium* of Roman London. He argues that these rights were unique and extended back beyond the conquest to the Saxon period. In Wheeler's view the Chiltern Grim's Ditch became the northern boundary of the post-Roman territory based on London. Wheeler also linked in the *Faesten dic* in Kent and the Surrey dykes as the south and western boundaries of this power based on the city of London. The Middlesex Grim's Ditch was also considered as a part of this system.

Wheeler notes that the entire Grim's Ditch lies on clay subsoil like the similar Middlesex Grim's Ditch. This means the ditch keeps consistent clay subsoil on the London side. The ditches stop where the poorer soils start. For Wheeler this meant that the Dyke had to be post-Roman as even the Belgic invaders were not able to work lower lying soils in river valleys. 'Our dykes can at least have nothing to do with prehistoric Britain.'

Until 'Saxon colonists swarmed up the rivers and cleared the valley-floors for settlement and tillage' these soils were not settled so the dykes must be Saxon constructions. For Wheeler, like Crawford, the Chiltern Grim's ditches must be part of a single system: 'Their essential unity is disguised by their intermittency'. Wheeler claims, contrary to Crawford, that the ditch is on the London side of the bank, so the ditches face towards London, and for Wheeler, they must be built by Saxon settlers from the north and north-west, as a defence against a still powerful political entity based in London.

The Grim's Ditch in Middlesex is also brought into the dyke system but Wheeler is never clear whether this is a later development when the Saxon settlers have moved closer to London or a deep penetration of Saxons along the valley bottom.

Excavations since the time of Wheeler and Crawford have exploded the idea of a single post-Roman earthwork in the Chilterns. In 1963 J. Dyer argues that the Chiltern Grim's Ditch is Iron Age, not Dark Age in date, though he still argues that it is a single monument (J. Dyer, 'The Chiltern Grim's Ditch'). Dyer shows that the ditch is often on the upper slope to the bank making it more like a boundary, not a defence. Dyer adds in two sections of dyke to the monument – one near Whipsnade and another near Dunstable – but removes the monument on Berkhamsted Common from the main Grim's Ditch. Both of these sections appear to be cut by Roman roads, making the whole monument prehistoric. There is also a new detached section at Grim's Dell. Dyer relates the Grim's Ditch to similar dykes at Beech's Bottom and Prae Wood near St Albans. Dyer sees the ditch as a boundary of the Catuvellauni against 'Belgic' settlers at St Albans.

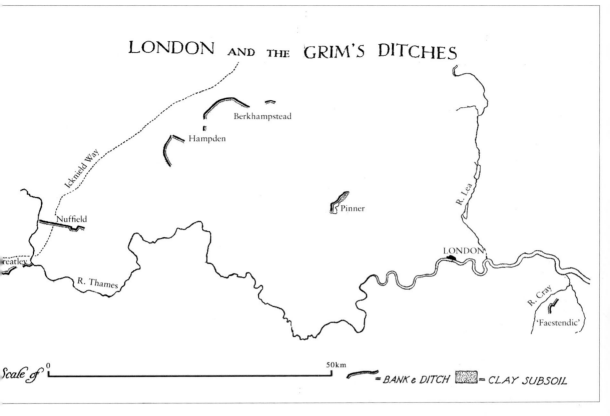

Map 32: London and the Grim's Ditches.

New excavations in the 1980s showed that the archaeology of Grim's Dyke was much more complicated than suggested by either Dyer or Crawford. A section of the Grim's Dyke on the Pitstone Hills was excavated (Davis, 1981). 'The course of the new ditch, confirmed by the aerial photograph, does not link happily with hitherto recorded lengths.' Davies suggests the Chiltern Grim's Ditch is not a system but a series of ditches that developed over time as agricultural boundaries.

The modern view is that the dykes mark out territories across the belt of lighter soils and have survived where other territorial boundaries have been ploughed away. It is more likely that the 'Chiltern Grim's Ditch' is not a single monument, built to a single plan but instead is a collection of separate local monuments built at different times and only seen as a single monument because of the common name used for different monuments.

There is a whole set of ditches that run north to south across the line of the 'Icknield Way', including the Dray's Ditches, Telegraph Hill, the dyke at Deadman's Hill at Sandon in Hertfordshire and the Mile Ditches at Royston in Hertfordshire. The 'Chiltern Grim's Ditch' is just the south western part of these series ditches. These eastern series of ditches have been excavated and all shown to be Iron Age.

THE BELGIC INVASION

These eighteenth- and nineteenth-century antiquarians tried to fit the monuments they saw in the landscape into the knowledge of ancient Britain gathered from their reading of classical texts. Julius Caesar had described a people called the Belgae, a confederation of Gaulish tribes. One member of the confederation was the *Suessiones* who within living memory, as Caesar put it, had a king who exercised power in Britain as well as in Gaul. A mixture of Caesar, archaeology and coin studies led to the idea that southern Britain was invaded a number of times by Belgic tribes. The consensus view was of a series of invasions from the continent from 150 BC onwards, with large-scale population movements after 50 BC as a direct effect of Caesar's wars in Gaul.

The idea of a Belgic Invasion persisted for a long time though the details were modified over time. One of the innovations that the Belgae are supposed to have brought with them was a heavier plough that could work some clay soils but only on plateaus, not lower lying soils in river valleys. This meant that any dykes found on heavier low-lying soils must be Roman or later. The modern view has changed and the ideal of a series of invasions causing massive change in the Iron Age has been rejected in favour of slow cultural change caused by trading contacts.

The replacement of curving Iron Age dykes that followed the contours with straighter dykes was also attributed to the Belgae, which led to some problems, for example the Iron Age dyke on Minchinhampton Common near Cirencester was a linear monument but 'as yet, however, no true Belgic material has been found in Minchinhampton' (Royal Commission on Historical Monuments, England). Also James Dyer in 'The Chiltern Grim's Ditch' stated, 'The layout of the Grim's Ditch as a series of arcs or scallops does not appear elsewhere in dykes of known or acceptable Belgic origin.'

GAZETTEER OF THE DYKES

This is a list of the dykes that have once been suggested as being post-Roman in date. Some of them now have evidence that they are prehistoric in date and others are still undated. The list is ordered by modern administrative county. The larger dykes that span several counties are noted where they appear in each county. Only dykes where there are physical remains on the ground have been included and sites where the only evidence is a place name have been ignored.

ENGLAND

Bath and North East Somerset

West Wansdyke
Post-Roman
The West Wansdyke runs from Maes Knoll in the west to Horsecombe in the east and is about 14 km long including gaps. The dyke runs close to or includes the defences of two Iron Age hillforts, Maes Knoll and Stantonbury. It has been suggested that the dyke runs further west than Maes Knoll, possibly as far as the Bristol Channel but this has never been confirmed.
References:
Erskine
Fox & Fox
Gardiner
Iles
Ordnance Survey

Bedfordshire

Dray's Ditches
Prehistoric

Dray's Ditches is a triple ditch system about 1 km long and running at right angles to the 'Icknield Way'. This was excavated in 1958 to test if it was late Roman or early Saxon in date, on analogy with the Cambridgeshire Dykes. The triple ditch system had V-shaped ditches, with evidence of an extensive palisade between the central and the southern ditch. All ditches had extensive Iron Age sherds in the ditch fill.

References:

J. F. Dyer

Berkshire

Crookham Dykes
Prehistoric

Crookham Common is 3–4 km east of Greenham Common has several earthworks. There are five possible dykes on Crookham Common, four certain and one earthwork which is a bank between two ditches, more probably prehistoric than post-Roman. Three dykes have ditches on the western side.

References:

O'Neil & Peake, 'A Linear Earthwork on Greenham Common Berkshire'

O'Neil, 'The Silchester Region in the 5th & 6th centuries AD'

Bury's Bank
Prehistoric

Bury's Bank was built on Greenham Common. This dyke was destroyed during the construction of Greenham Common airfield in the Second World War but fortunately excavated in advance of destruction.

References:

O'Neil & Peake, 'A Linear Earthwork on Greenham Common Berkshire'

O'Neil, 'The Silchester Region in the 5th & 6th centuries AD'

Grim's Bank 1
Prehistoric

The Grim's Bank 1 between Aldermaston and Padworth runs between the Roman road from Silchester to Bath to the Roman road between Silchester and Dorchester on Thames, it is a straight line ditch. Excavation found the bank 1.0 m high, 9.40 m wide.

References:

Astill

Cockin

O'Neil, 'Grim's Bank Padworth Berkshire'
O'Neil, 'The Silchester Region in the 5th & 6th centuries AD'

Grim's Bank 2
Unknown

Grim's Bank 2 appears to connect to Grim's Bank 1. Grim's Bank 2 possibly relates to an Iron Age hilltop site at Mortimer Common. The dyke was prehistoric and possibly reused and extended to form a post-Roman defence.
References:
O'Neil, 'The Silchester Region in the 5th & 6th centuries AD'
Cockin

Grim's Bank Aldworth
Prehistoric

Included as part of the 'Chiltern Grim's Ditch' by Crawford. Ford's excavations produced Roman material from the ditch and a *terminus ante quem* in the later third century AD.
References:
O. G. Crawford, 'The Chiltern Grim's Ditches'
Ford, 'Linear Earthworks on the Berkshire Downs'
O'Neil, 'The Silchester Region in the 5th & 6th centuries AD'

Grim's Ditch
Prehistoric

The Berkshire Grim's Ditch is the longest of the Wessex linear earthworks. It runs along the escarpment of the Berkshire Downs, overlooking the Vale of the White Horse. Limited excavation in 1930 suggested a Roman or post-Roman date, and O. G. S. Crawford promoted it as a post-Roman earthwork. Ford's excavation in the 1980s showed the dyke was constructed in the Bronze Age.
References:
Ford, 'Field Work and Excavation on the Berkshire Grims Ditch'
Ford, 'Linear Earthworks on the Berkshire Downs'

Wansdyke
Unknown

There is a possible section of Wansdyke in the parish of Inkpen, just into Berkshire, situated close to a road called Old Dyke Lane. Crawford believed the Wansdyke extended east from Savernake Forest, incorporating the Bedwyn Dykes and this section of dyke. An enclosure award of 1735 mentions this as 'Wans Dyke'. It is also referred to 'readan dic' the Red Ditch in a ninth-century charter.
References:
O. G. Crawford, *Archaeology in the Field*
Fox & Fox

Buckinghamshire

Grim's Ditch Hampden
Prehistoric

This substantial linear earthwork stretches from Park Wood to Hampden House and is about 5 km long. This formed part of Crawford's 'Chiltern Grim's Ditch'. Later work suggests that it is more likely to be Bronze or Iron Age than post-Roman in date.
References:
R. Bradley, 'The South Oxfordshire Grim's Ditch and its Significance'
O. G. Crawford, 'The Chiltern Grim's Ditches'
Davis
J. F. Dyer
J. Dyer, 'The Chiltern Grim's Ditch'
Hughes
R. E. Wheeler

Grim's Ditch Misenden
Prehistoric

Another stretch of dyke running from the Missenden Valley to the Lea. It once formed part of Crawford's 'Chiltern Grim's Ditch' but more likely to be Bronze or Iron Age than post-Roman in date.
References:
O. G. Crawford, 'The Chiltern Grim's Ditches'
Davis
J. F. Dyer
J. Dyer, The Chiltern Grim's Ditch
Hughes
Ordnance Survey
R. E. Wheeler

Grim's Ditch King's Ash to County Boundary

The third section of Grim's Ditch in Buckinghamshire runs from King's Ash to the county boundary with Hertfordshire where it continues across the border to Berkhamsted, see Hertfordshire. Again this was part of Crawford's 'Chiltern Grim's Ditch' but more likely to be Bronze or Iron Age than post-Roman in date.
References:
O. G. Crawford, 'The Chiltern Grim's Ditches'
Davis
J. F. Dyer
J. Dyer, 'The Chiltern Grim's Ditch'
Hughes
Ordnance Survey
R. E. Wheeler

Cambridgeshire

Bran or Heydon Ditch
Post-Roman

This dyke now only survives as a field boundary. Excavation has shown the ditch was cut 1.8 m deep into the natural chalk, with width of 5.75 m. The berm was 1.5 m, between the bank and ditch and the bank was 8.5 m, wide. The bank was recorded as being 2.1 m high in the nineteenth century. Excavation shows a possible revetment along the bank.
References:
J. Dyer, *Southern England: An Archaeological Guide*
C. Fox, 'The Archaeology of the Cambridge Region'
Hope-Taylor & Hill
Lethbridge, 'The Car Dyke, the Cambridgeshire Ditches and the Anglo-Saxons'
Lethbridge, 'The Riddle of the Dykes'
Malim, 'New Evidence on the Cambridgeshire Dykes and Warstead Street Roman Road'
Ordnance Survey

Brent Ditch
Post-Roman

This is also known as the Pampisford Ditch. The Brent Ditch survives as an upstanding section of 2.3 km at the north end while the southern section only survives as a small ground depression. No evidence of a massive bank, but slight ridges on either side of the ditch. The ditch was 3 m deep and 2.6 m wide at the base and 4.5 m wide at the top. It was built in a single phase and shows no evidence of cleaning or re-cutting.
References:
J. Dyer, *Southern England: An Archaeological Guide*
C. Fox, 'The Archaeology of the Cambridge Region'
Hope-Taylor & Hill
Lethbridge, 'The Car Dyke, the Cambridgeshire Ditches and the Anglo-Saxons'
Lethbridge, 'The Riddle of the Dykes'
Malim, 'New Evidence on the Cambridgeshire Dykes and Warstead Street Roman Road'
Ordnance Survey

Devil's Dyke
Post-Roman

The Devil's Dyke is the best preserved of all the Cambridgeshire Dykes. The dyke is 11 km long and the central section is straight and impressive in the flat landscape of the fens. The dyke runs from Woodditton in the south to Reach on the Fen edge in the north. The angle of the bank means it is very stable and has eroded only slightly. The bank and ditch still present a formidable obstacle.

References:
J. Dyer, *Southern England: An Archaeological Guide*
C. Fox, 'The Archaeology of the Cambridge Region'
Hope-Taylor and Hill
Lethbridge, 'The Car Dyke, the Cambridgeshire Ditches and the Anglo-Saxons'
Lethbridge, 'The Riddle of the Dykes'
Malim, 'New evidence on the Cambridgeshire Dykes and Warstead Street Roman Road'
Ordnance Survey
Royal Commission on Historical Monuments (England)

Fleam Dyke
Post-Roman

The Fleam Dyke is in three parts. The main section is also called the Balsham Ditch and runs northwards from Oxcroft Farm near Balsham to Shardelow's Well. Then there is the 'northern extension' from Shardelow's Well to Great Wilbraham Fen. Then High Ditch at Fen Ditton may be part of the Fleam Dyke or could be a separate monument of prehistoric date. The most likely date for the Fleam Dyke proper is the early Saxon period. The bank was raised in a number of stages, unlike the other Cambridgeshire Dykes. There is a possible post-hole for a revetment at the front of the bank. At the southern end the Fleam Dyke only survives as a hedge bank.
References:
J. Dyer, *Southern England: An Archaeological Guide*
C. Fox, 'The Archaeology of the Cambridge Region'
Hope-Taylor and Hill
Lethbridge, 'The Car Dyke, the Cambridgeshire Ditches and the Anglo-Saxons'
Lethbridge, 'The Riddle of the Dykes'
Malim, 'New evidence on the Cambridgeshire Dykes and Warstead Street Roman Road'
Ordnance Survey
Royal Commission on Historical Monuments (England)

Cornwall

Giant's Hedge
Unknown

The Giant's Hedge runs from Lerryn to Looe between two rivers. It survives in a variable state; some sections are well preserved while others have been destroyed. The Bank is up to 4 m wide and up to 2.5 m high. The ditch is on the north side though it cannot be seen along all sections of dyke. The course of the dyke is uncertain in several places.
References:
O. G. Crawford, 'The Work of Giants'
Page
Ordnance Survey

Bolster Bank
Unknown

This is an earthwork of 3.2 km in length that cuts off St Agnes' beacon in parish of St Agnes. From the top of the bank to the base of the ditch is about 3.5 m. Bolster Bank encloses an area of 5 sq. km. Legend has it that a giant called Bolster built it, forcing St Agnes to help him carry the stones. No evidence for a date but O. G. S. Crawford suggested it was post-Roman.
References:
Johnson
Ordnance Survey

Giant's Grave
Unknown

O. G. S. Crawford suggested the Giant's Grave was post-Roman. It has also been suggested that this was a civil war entrenchment. It possibly once stretched from coast to coast, cutting off the Penwith peninsula.
References:
O. G. Crawford, 'The Work of Giants'
Ordnance Survey

Derbyshire

Calver Cross Ridge Dyke
Unknown

The Calver Cross Ridge Dyke lies at the eastern end of Longstone Edge and is now cut in two by mineral workings. The height of the bank is about 2 m. Width of dyke and ditch together is about 14 m. There is no dating evidence and it has been suggested as post-Roman by analogy with the Grey Ditch.
References:
Hart

The Grey Ditch
Post-Roman

The Grey Ditch was built at right angles across a Roman road. Excavations have shown that the bank was about 8 m wide at the base and survived up to a height of 1.2 m. The ditch showed evidence of up to five re-cuts. The bank lay over a plough soil, which contained sherds of Roman-British pottery.
References:
Hart
O'Neil, Grey Ditch, Bradwell, Derbyshire
Ordnance Survey

Longstone Edge Cross Ridge Dyke

Longstone Edge Cross Ridge Dyke lies on the eastern edge of Longstone Edge. It is proposed as a post-Roman dyke on analogy with the Grey Ditch. There is no dating evidence. The dyke is a double dyke in the south and a single dyke in the north. The bank is up to 1 m high.

Dorset

Battery Banks and Worgret Dykes

Unknown

Four dykes are found to the east of Wareham, between the River Piddle or Trent and the River Frome. If the Worgret dykes are Romano-British then Battery Banks which post-dates the Worgret Dykes could be post-Roman.

References:

Coe & Hawkes

Bokerley Dyke

Post-Roman

The earthwork is about 6 km long and runs north-east across Cramborne Chase from West Woodyates to Martin Wood. It blocks the Ackling Dyke Roman road. Away from the road Bokerley Dyke is still an impressive monument. Bokerley Dyke still marks the county boundary between Dorset and Hampshire. Bokerly Dyke was an older spelling.

References:

H. C. Bowen

C. F. Hawkes

Ordnance Survey

Pitt Rivers, 'Excavations in Bokerly and Wansdyke Dorset and Wilts 1888 – 1891'

P. A. Rahtz

Sumner

Comb's Ditch

Post-Roman

Comb's Ditch is on Charlton Down, south of Blandford Forum. It was at least 6.4 km long but now only 4.4 km survives. It still forms the parish boundary between several Dorset parishes. In the nineteenth century it was thought that it formed a second line of defence to Bokerley Dyke. It has several phases and is likely to be an Iron Age dyke reused in the post-Roman period.

References:

Ordnance Survey

Pitt Rivers, 'Excavations in Bokerly and Wansdyke Dorset and Wilts 1888 – 1891'

P. J. Fowler, 'Interim Report on an Excavation in Combs Ditch Dorset, 1964'

Sumner

Grim's Ditch Cramborne Chase
Prehistoric

Grim's Ditch on Cramborne Chase is a prehistoric dyke probably of Bronze Age date. Some antiquarians such as John Aubrey confused it with Bokerley Dyke.
References:
Piggot

Gloucestershire

The Bulwarks
Prehistoric

The Bulwarks is a linear earthwork on Minchinhampton Common, about 13 km west of Cirencester. Excavation in 1937 by Clifford found Iron Age material from the bank and Roman pottery in the ditch fill. Clifford linked the Bulwarks and a further earthwork at Rodborough to Amberley Camp, an Iron Age hillfort. The Bulwarks seems to be a single phase monument of around the first half of the first century AD, though it has been recently suggested by Reid that it is a post-Roman boundary against Anglo-Saxon expansion into the Cotswolds.
References:
Clifford
Reid
Royal Commission on Historical Monuments (England)

Bagendon Dykes
Prehistoric

O. G. S. Crawford considered the Bagendon Dykes to be post-Roman: 'The Bagendon dykes still await excavation, and indeed description, but must surely be closely connected with Cirencester, and probably with the battle of Deorham (Dyrham, north of Bath) in 577 which led to the capture of Cirencester'. Excavation has shown this area is an *oppidum*, the Iron Age predecessor to the Roman town of Cirencester.
References:
O. G. Crawford, *Archaeology in the Field*

Offa's Dyke
Post-Roman

Offa's Dyke in Gloucestershire consists of substantial earthworks along the left bank of the River Wye from the border with Herefordshire in the north to Sedbury in the south above the confluence of the Wye with the Severn. The Wye still forms the border between England and Wales. Hill & Worthington have challenged Fox's claim that these earthworks are part of Offa's Dyke but there is a medieval reference to these earthworks as 'Offediche'.

References:
Bapty
Currie, Herbert & Baggs
C. Fox, *Offa's Dyke*
Hill, 'Offa's & Wat's Dykes'
Hill & Worthington, *Offa's Dyke History and Guide*

Greater London

Grim's Ditch, Pear Wood, Brockley Hill
Post-Roman
The earthwork in Pear Wood may be the eastern end of the Middlesex Grim's Dyke that runs from Pinner to Harrow. Alternatively it may be a separate monument. The monument is called 'Grymesdich' in a document of AD 1535. The Pear Wood earthwork runs at a right angle to Watling Street, the main Roman road between London and St Albans. The earthwork does not go right up to Watling Street ending about 180 m west of Watling Street, and there is no evidence of any continuation on the east side of Watling Street. The earthwork is about 27 m wide, and the ditch is V-shaped, 4 m wide and 1.5 to 1.8 m deep.
References:
Bowlt
Castle
Thompson, 'Harrow AD 400–AD 1066'
Thompson, 'Harrow in the Roman Period'

Grim's Dyke Pinner to Harrow Middlesex
Unknown
The Grims's Dyke runs from Pinner to Harrow Weald Common and is known as the Grim's Ditch. It has been badly damaged by housing development in the twentieth century. It may have joined up with the Pear Wood dyke. Recent excavation on another detached section of dyke in Ruislip suggests that the Grim's Dyke may once have extended further to the south and be post-Roman in date.
References:
Bowlt
Braun
Ellis
Stone
Thompson, 'Harrow AD 400–AD 1066'
Thompson, 'Harrow in the Roman Period'

Greater Manchester

The Nico Ditch
Unknown

This is a curving linear earthwork to the south and east of Manchester city centre. The ditch is on the south side of low bank 8 km long between two marshy areas, Hough's Moss to the west and Ashton Moss to the east. The first mention of the dyke is of 'Mykel Ditch' in deed of around AD 1200. The origin of the name Nico Ditch is disputed, Nico or Nicleer is the most common spelling of the name. As the original name was Mickle it is most likely to be from the Anglo-Saxon 'mickle' or great. The great would refer to the length of the ditch not its size and be similar to early references to the Devil's Dyke in Cambridgeshire as the 'great ditch'.

The function of the dyke is unknown; it could be defensive, for administration or drainage, all of which have been suggested as theories. The dyke does mark parish and estate boundaries. The dyke is not well sited for defence and never seems to have had a large bank. Limited excavations have found no trace of a bank in several places thought this may be due to the extensive damage done to the dyke by development. Excavations have not found any evidence for dating, only post-medieval artefacts have been found in the ditch fills. There is no evidence for an immediate post-Roman date.
References:
Ordnance Survey

Hampshire

The Devil's Ditch
Prehistoric

The OS map shows a Devil's Ditch in Hampshire. It may be the Devil's Ditch mentioned by O. G. S. Crawford in *The Andover District*. There is no evidence that it is post-Roman and is more likely to be one of a number of prehistoric Devil's Ditches in Hampshire.
References:
O. G. Crawford, *The Andover District*
Ordnance Survey

The Festean Dic
Unknown

Hogg suggested the dyke called the *Festean Dic* on Hartford Bridge Flats in north-east Hampshire was post-Roman in date. Others have suggested that it is a late medieval hundred boundary. Recent work by the North East Hampshire Historical and Archaeological Society has shown there are a series of dykes and terraces that overlie a possible Roman road. There is no evidence for dating and no excavation has taken place, but the positioning is suggestive. Without further work this dyke must remain in the uncertain category.

References:
Grinsell
A. H. Hogg
Whaley

The Froxfield Long Entrenchments
Unknown

In Froxfield, close to Petersfield there are a whole series of earthworks. Coffin suggested one of them, known as the Froxfield long entrenchments, was post-Roman and formed the boundary of a Jutish sub-kingdom. There is no evidence for the date of any of the Froxfield dykes and the idea of the dyke being the boundary of an Anglo-Saxon kingdom must remain speculation.
References:
Coffin

Herefordshire

Offa's Dyke
Post-Roman

The continuous line of Offa's Dyke ends at Rushock Hill. There are fragments of dyke along the River Wye which Fox saw as a continuation of Offa's Dyke but these have been disputed by Hill & Worthington.
References:
C. Fox, *Offa's Dyke*
Hill, 'Offa's & Wat's Dykes'
Hill & Worthington, *Offa's Dyke History and Guide*
Ordnance Survey

Perrystone Court
Unknown

The dyke at Perrystone Court, near Perrystone east of the River Wye and west of Yatton Wood was regarded as a 'Magonsaeton' work by Fox but it has not been excavated. It lies very close to the dyke at Yatton Wood.

Yatton Wood and Fox's work are not part of Offa's Dyke, but have not been excavated so their date has not been confirmed.
References:
C. Fox, *Offa's Dyke*

Rowe Ditch, Pembridge
Post-Roman

The Rowe Ditch is a substantial dyke to the east of Pembridge. Length is 3.5 km with a ditch on the western side and extends on both sides of the River Arrow. The

Rowe Ditch lies over an excavated ditch which has produced Iron Age and Roman pottery, supporting an Anglo-Saxon date. Sometimes has been considered as a second alignment of Offa's dyke. The Rowe ditch should not be confused with the two earthworks called the Row (or Rowe) Ditch in the city of Hereford which are part of the medieval defences of the city.

References:

C. Fox, *Offa's Dyke*

Rodd

Yatton Wood Dyke

Unknown

This dyke is on the south side of Yatton Wood. It lies close to the Perrrystone Court Dyke. Now very badly damaged, it has a ditch on the south side. It was regarded as a 'Magonsaeton' work by Fox but it has not been excavated.

References:

C. Fox, *Offa's Dyke*

Hertfordshire

Grim's Ditch Berkhamsted

Prehistoric

This dyke formed part of Crawford's 'Chiltern Grim's Ditch'. It is Bronze or Iron Age in date. This part of Grim's Ditch runs from Woodcock Hill east of Berkhamsted to Longcroft Farm on the county boundary and carries on into Buckinghamshire.

References:

O. G. Crawford, 'The Chiltern Grim's Ditches'

Davis

J. F. Dyer

J. Dyer, 'The Chiltern Grim's Ditch'

Hughes

Ordnance Survey

R. E. Wheeler

Grim's Ditch Berkhamsted Common

Prehistoric

There are two sections earthwork called Grim's Ditch on Berkhamsted Common. It does not follow the contours like the rest of the Chiltern 'Grim's Ditch' and is much bigger in size. The Hertfordshire HER suggests it is Iron Age and comparable with the Iron Age dykes of the St Albans area.

References:

O. G. Crawford, 'The Chiltern Grim's Ditches'

Davis

J. F. Dyer
J. Dyer, 'The Chiltern Grim's Ditch'
Hughes
Ordnance Survey
R. E. Wheeler

Mile Ditches
Prehistoric
The Mile Ditches were first noted in 1886. They are 2.5 km west of Royston and run from Therfield Heath northwards to Wellhead Springs. When Beldam first saw them they consisted of three parallel ditches and four banks. By the 1930s the ditches had been heavily ploughed and were mostly visible only as crop marks. The ditches were completely levelled by the 1940s. O. G. S. Crawford suggested they were post-Roman on analogy with the Chiltern Grim's Ditch. The dykes were believed to block the Icknield Way in the same way as the Cambridgeshire Dykes and the Chiltern Grim's Dyke. Excavation in the 1970s showed the ditches were most likely Iron Age in date. The total width of the banks and ditches was about 22 m. Excavation suggested that the ditches had developed over a period of time, though the levelling of the ditches had removed any stratigraphical relationship between them. Ditches had filled up over a long period of time, with Roman and medieval material in the top ditch fills. Parallel to Dray's Ditches in Bedfordshire in form.
References:
Beldam
Burleigh
O. G. Crawford, 'The Mile Ditches at Royston'

Kent

Faestendic
Unknown
The *Faestendic* or *Faesten Dic* is situated in Joyden's Wood, near Bexley in Kent. The wood contains a number of earthworks of unknown dates. The dyke runs roughly north to south, zigzagging for 1.6 km. The ditch is on the west side of the bank. The ditch is up to 8 m wide and now up to 2 m deep. The bank is up to 1.5 m high and 2.5 m wide. The dyke has been identified with the one mentioned in an Anglo-Saxon charter of AD 814 which describes the boundaries of Bexley, where it is referred to as the *faestendic*.
References:
H. A. Hogg
Ordnance Survey

Leicestershire

King Lud's Entrenchment
Unknown

King Lud's Entrenchment or Intrenchment is also known as King Lud's Bank and was one of the Dark Age dykes, listed by Crawford in the Ordnance Survey's original Dark Age map. The dyke still forms the county boundary between Leicestershire and Lincolnshire. Once considered as post-Roman, opinion has swung to regard this monument as part of the 'Jurassic spine', a system of prehistoric ditches and earthworks that runs from Northamptonshire through Lincolnshire to the Humber. The dyke has not been excavated.
References:
Ordnance Survey

Norfolk

Bichamditch or Devil's Dyke
Unknown

Bichamditch or Devil's Dyke is assumed to be post-Roman but no firm dating evidence has been found. It runs in a straight line for 8 km from Beachamwell to Narborough. Close to the end of the Bichamditch is the Iron Age hillfort of Narborough Camp. The relationship between the two is unknown. This dyke is east facing not west facing as shown on the OS maps.
References:
Ordnance Survey
Wade-Martins

Bunn's Bank
Unknown

Bun's Bank may be post-Roman. This dyke may be projected to end near a Roman road and is linked to the 'Double Banks'. Much of the earthwork was used as a medieval park boundary, and the earthwork now has a ditch on both sides, and it is not possible to tell if this was its original form. No firm dating evidence for this dyke.

Devil's Ditch
Iron Age

The dyke is located near Garboldisham and runs from the Little Ouse northwards, where it is used as a parish boundary, for about one kilometre where it fades out. An excavation and watching brief by the Norfolk Archaeological Unit in 2007 sampled the ditch for OSL dating. The results suggested the ditch was dug in the Iron Age and re-cut during the Middle Saxon period.

References:
Ordnance Survey
Wade-Martins

Double Banks
Unknown

A single bank with a ditch on either side, suggested that it may be post-Roman. No dating evidence for the dyke. Linked to Bunn's Bank at the north end and used as the boundary of a deer park in the medieval period.

Fossditch
Post-Roman

The Fossditch or Foss Ditch runs between the Wissey and the Ouse, blocking off the land between the two rivers. The dyke faces east not west as shown on the OS map. It was described as 'much destroyed' even in 1854 but Clarke doubts it was much longer than the 8.8 km now existing. The name Fossditch was used from AD 1100, early names were le Burghdyk, Burdicke and Burdyckway. The Devil's Ditch is an eighteenth-century name. It lies over a soil full of Roman pottery dating between the early second and late fourth century.
References:
Babington
Ordnance Survey
Clarke
Wade-Martins

Launditch
Unknown

The Launditch was at least 6 km long but only 0.9 km survives as an upstanding monument. It is straight in the central section and curves eastwards at each end. An unpublished 1992 excavation by the Norfolk Archaeology Unit suggests it is Iron Age in date.
References:
Ordnance Survey
Wade-Martins

The Panworth Ditch
Unknown

The Panworth Ditch or Devil's Dyke is a curvilinear earthwork that lies on a possible Roman road. It is built in a hollow and does not have a commanding position, and there is no excavation evidence to confirm or deny a post-Roman date. Wade-Martins dated the Panworth Ditch by comparison with the Launditch, which may be Iron Age. This dyke is not shown on the Ordnance Survey maps of the Dark Ages. The Panworth Ditch faces west.

References:
Wade-Martins

North Yorkshire

Dane's Dyke
Prehistoric

It has been suggested that the Dane's Dyke may be post-Roman. Dane's Dyke cuts off Flamborough Head, making a natural strong point. A section dug by Pitt Rivers in 1879 found only Neolithic flints in the bank. The date of the dyke depends on the accuracy of this section.

References:
Pitt Rivers, 'On Excavations in the Earthwork Called Dane's Dyke at Flamborough in October, 1879; and on the Earthworks of the Yorkshire Wolds'
P. Rahtz

The Rudgate Dyke
Unknown

There is some confusion about the possible Rudgate Dyke. In 'Roman Roads West of Tadcaster', Ramm describes an excavation on the Rudgate, the Roman road which runs from Aldborough to join the road known as the Roman Ridge. A single trench was dug in Toulston Park in 1962. The excavation did not find the agger of the Roman road but did find two parallel ditches. The western ditch, 3 m wide and 1.3 m to 1.5 m deep, was rock-cut. The presence of silting lines in the ditch fill showed there had once been a bank on the west side of the ditch. Ramm suggested this was part of a defensive earthwork facing east, using the agger of the Roman road as part of the bank. No dating evidence was recovered for this possible bank, apart from it post-dating the Roman road.

References:
Ramm
Wilmott

The Scot's Dyke
Iron Age

The Scot's Dyke (also Scots Dyke or Scots Dike) runs from the Swale to the Tees for 14 km. The dyke runs from Eastby on the Swale to a point close to the *oppidum* of Stanwick. On the south side of the A66 the dyke survives as an earthwork for 250 m. The bank up to 1.5 m high and 10 m wide, with the ditch on the east side being 7 m wide and 1 m deep. A counterscarp bank on the east side of the ditch is up to 5 m wide. The dyke is 7.6 m above ditch level at the highest point, about 1.5 m taller than the earthworks at the site of Stanwick. A gap in the dyke to the south of the present A66 may be the gap through which the Roman road passed if it is original. Excavation

showed a rock cut ditch 4 m wide. OSL and archaeomagnetic dating showed the ditch filled up in the first century AD, suggesting the Scot's Dyke was built in the late Iron Age.
References:
Clarkson
Karloukovski & Hounslow
Northern Archaeological Associates
Ordnance Survey
Oxford Archaeology North
Smith

Northumberland

The Black Dyke
Prehistoric
The Black Dyke is an earthwork east of Housesteads. There have been claims that it is a post-Roman boundary between Bernicia and Rheged. The dyke is cut by Hadrian's Wall's making it prehistoric. The Black Dyke has been used to link the Catrail in southern Scotland to the Scot's Dyke in North Yorkshire.
References:
Grigg
Spain
Wooler

Oxfordshire

Aves Ditch
Prehistoric
The Aves ditch is a straight dyke in north Oxfordshire. The ditch is on the west side of the bank. In parts the ditch is cut into the limestone bedrock. The excavator suggested Aves Ditch may originally have had a hedge running along the top of the bank. Iron Age in date but had an Anglo-Saxon burial cut into the ditch.
References:
Sauer

The North Oxfordshire Grim's Ditch
Prehistoric
This is a complex of earthworks to the north-west of Oxford, once suggested by O. G. S. Crawford to be post-Roman in date. There are a large number of discontinuous earthworks. The dyke is composed of two circuits of earthworks. The relationship between the two circuits is disputed. The length of the earthworks making up circuit

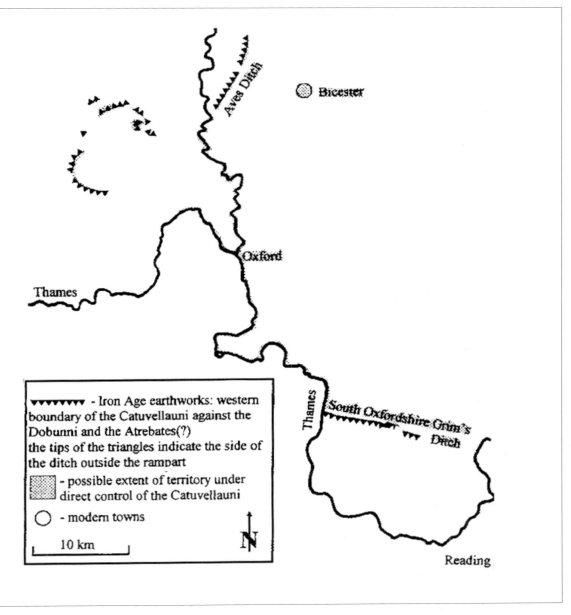

Map 33: Ave's Ditch and other Iron Age earthworks in Oxfordshire after Sauer.

one is about 10 km while circuit two has about 20 km of earthworks. The large gaps between the earthworks may be because the dyke was never completed. The whole complex covers an area of around 80 sq. km. The ditch is on the outside of the bank, so the monument faces outward. A possible palisade trench was found in front of the ditch at some points but not at others. The same was true of a possible counterscarp to the bank. Material from excavation has shown the dyke was constructed in the late Iron Age and went out of use in the early Roman period. It has been suggested that the North Oxfordshire Grim's Ditch is an *oppidum*, but there does not appear to be a central settlement within the area defined by the ditches and it would be the largest monument of its type in Britain.

References:

Copeland

O. G. Crawford, 'Grim's Ditch in Wychwood Oxon'

Fine

Sauer

South Oxford Grim's Ditch
Unknown

The South Oxford Grim's Ditch is also known as the Mongwell Ditch. O. G. S. Crawford considered it as a part of the Chiltern Grim's Ditch. Bradley suggested it was more likely to be prehistoric. There have been no excavations to prove the date of the dyke.

References:

R. Bradley, 'The South Oxfordshire Grim's Ditch and its Significance'

O. G. Crawford, 'The Chiltern Grim's Ditches'

Ordnance Survey

Shropshire

Lower Short Ditch
Post-Roman

This dyke runs across the border between Powys and Shropshire with the majority of the dyke in Shropshire. It is 800 m long with about 770 m in Shropshire and only 30 m in Powys. The bank is 8 m wide, the ditch 3 m wide, and a height of 2.5 m from ditch bottom to top of bank. It has been dated as part of the Short Dykes project and gave a radiocarbon date of cal. AD 410–590.

References:

Hankinson & Caseldine

Offa's Dyke

There are three sections of Offa's Dyke in Shropshire as the dyke crosses the county boundary into Powys and back into Shropshire. Here is the central section of Offa's Dyke that runs along the uplands.

References:

C. Fox, *Offa's Dyke*

Hill & Worthington, *Offa's Dyke History and Guide*

Wat's Dyke

Wat's Dyke in Shropshire runs from Maesbury Hill past Old Oswestry Hillfort to a point south of Glynmorlas where the dyke disappears at the Chirk Gap, before reappearing in Wrexham.

References:

C. Fox, *Offa's Dyke*

Hannaford

H. H. Andersen

Hayes & Malim

Hill & Worthington, *Offa's Dyke History and Guide*

Malim, 'The Origins and Design of Linear Earthworks in the Welsh Marches'

Somerset

Ponter's Ball

Medieval

This dyke was listed on the 1966 OS map as a 'Celtic' post-Roman monument. Excavation in 1970 showed the bank overlay soil containing prehistoric and medieval potsherds.

References:

Ordnance Survey

South Yorkshire

The Roman Ridge

Unknown

The total length of this dyke is about 27 km. The earthwork begins in the outskirts of Sheffield, and follows the line of the Don valley to Kimberworth where it splits into two branches. One branch, the shorter one, goes to Swinton Common. The longer branch goes to Mexborough. The ends of the dyke are uncertain and there are a number of gaps which mean the exact route is uncertain. It is not known if any of these gaps are original. The form of the Roman Ridge is unique; no other dyke is known to have multiple branches. The Roman Ridge is first mentioned by Camden in his *Britannia* of 1586. Several excavations have failed to find any dating evidence for the Roman Ridge.

References:

Ashbee

Boldrini

Cronk, *Journey Along the Roman Ridge: Exploring the Purpose of South-West Yorkshire's Ancient Dykes*

Cronk, *South West Yorkshire's Roman Ridge: A Who-dug-it Mystery*

D. Green, 'The Roman Ridge Hill Top, Kimberworth near Rotherham'
Green & Preston, 'Two Excavations in the 'Roman Ridge' Dyke'
Preston
Riley

The Bar Dyke
Unknown

The Bar Dyke is 3 km north-west of Bradfield, on the east side of Broomhead Moor and about 400 m long. The bank is about 8 m wide and the ditch 7 m wide. The maximum height of the bank is about 1.5 m. The dyke is cut into three sections by track, and it is not known if the breaks are original. There is no dating evidence for this dyke and it is dated on comparison with other examples in Yorkshire. There is no dating evidence for this dyke and the post-Roman date was suggested by typological comparison with other examples in Yorkshire, which we have seen are more likely to be Iron Age in date. The Bar Dyke must remain in the unknown category until further evidence emerges.

Suffolk

The Black Ditches
Prehistoric

The Black Ditches is only a single ditch despite the name. It is in the parish of Cavenham in Suffolk between the River Lark and Cavenham Brook. About 1 km of ditch survives on a north-south alignment. A now detached length of the ditch forms the parish boundary between Cavenham and Lackford. The total length would be about 5.5 km assuming a continuous earthwork. A cleaning and recording exercise in 1992 where the ditch had been cut away for gravel extraction showed the dyke had a ditch on each side of the bank it was bivallate. Also late Iron Age pottery sherds were found in the eastern ditch. This strongly suggests an Iron Age date but does not prove it.
References:
Ordnance Survey

Surrey

Esher and Cobham Parish Boundary
Unknown

A bank and ditch across Esher Common marks the Esher and Cobham parish boundary. The Surrey Historic Environmental Record suggests this could be a Saxon boundary bank or earlier but there is no evidence for the date of this dyke.

Fullingadic
Unknown

The Fullingadic is mentioned in a charter of *c.* AD 672. This boundary dyke runs from the Thames across Wisley and Ockham Commons. It is very difficult to find the line of the Fullingadic on the ground and the Surrey Historic Environmental Record suggests that the Cobham and Ockham boundary, mentioned in a fourteenth-century document, might be the alignment of the dyke instead.

References:

Blair, 'Frithuwold's Kingdom and the Origin of Surrey'

Kent Surrey Boundary Ditch
Unknown

This is a cross-valley dyke 320 m long in Limpsfield on the Kent and Surrey boundary. It is undated but the Surrey Historic Environmental Record suggests it is early medieval.

Thames Ditton Ditch
Unknown

This is a linear earthwork running from the Thames to Surbiton Golf Club for 4 km. The Surrey Historic Environmental Record suggests either a Roman or prehistoric boundary. If this is the ditch referred in the name 'Long Ditton' and the name is Saxon then it must be pre-Saxon in date.

West Sussex

The Devil's Dyke and the Chichester Entrenchments
Iron Age

The Chichester entrenchments were first mentioned in documents of the thirteenth century. There are at least fifteen linear earthworks between the foot of the South Downs and Chichester Harbour. Theories about the date of the entrenchments ranged from Iron Age, Roman, to mark *centuriation* (land division) for the city of Chichester, to post-Roman. They lie to the north and north-east of the city of Chichester and the Entrenchments separate the entire coastal plain from the land to the north. Excavation showed that they are Iron Age in date.

References:

R. Bradley

Bedwin, 'Excavations at the Devil's Ditch, Boxgrove, West Sussex 1981'

Bedwin & Place, 'Late Iron Age and Romano-British occupation at Ounces Barn, Boxgrove, West Sussex; excavations 1982–83'

West Yorkshire

The West Yorkshire Grim's Ditch
Iron Age
The Grim's Ditch is a substantial dyke; excavated sections of the ditch are up to 19.15 m wide and up to 1.25 m deep, with the bank surviving to a height of up to 1.83 m and 18.30 m wide and about 10 km long. Cut into bedrock in some places. It is now badly damaged by development and fragmented. It was suggested as post-Roman in date because of the name Grim's Ditch. Between Leeds and Castleford it runs from Whinmoor to the River Aire. The ditch is on the east side. Excavations for the A1(M) upgrading showed it was Iron Age in date and filled up in the late Roman or post-Roman period.
References:
Roberts I & Berg
Wilmott

Becca Banks
Iron Age
Becca Banks is about 2.5 km long, with the bank up to 2 m high and the ditch 1.5 m deep. Becca Banks shows a small counterscarp on the ditch that is up to 1 m high. The modern village of Aberford has destroyed the eastern end of Becca Banks and so any relationship between the dyke and the line of the Roman road has been lost. The ditch is on the south side. Becca Banks is built over an Iron Age or early Roman enclosure. Radiocarbon dating showed the filling of the ditches to be late Roman.
References:
Alcock
Ordnance Survey
Roberts I & Berg

The Rein
Iron Age
The Rein or The Woodhouse Moor Rein is a straight line dyke to the south of the Cock Beck; it cuts through the South Dyke. Where it cuts the South Dyke it is now only 0.5 m high but further to the south survives as a bank 5 m high and 16 m wide with the ditch 9 m wide and 2 m deep. The Rein may have been built as a replacement for the South Dyke.
References:
Alcock
Ordnance Survey
Roberts I & Berg

The Ridge
The Ridge is to the west of Becca Banks by a wooded area. The west end of the Ridge appears to be unfinished. The Ridge and Becca Banks are sometimes just referred to

as Becca Banks. It is about 1 km long, along the scarp to the north of the Cock Beck. The ditch is still up to 3 m deep in places. The scarp and bank are about 3 m high.
References:
Alcock
Ordnance Survey
Roberts I & Berg

The South Dyke
Iron Age

A substantial monument on the scarp to the south of the Cock Beck the ditch is 1 m deep and 10 m wide and the bank up to 12 m high where it survives. The dyke curves at the western end. The western end of the dyke has been destroyed by the Aberford By-pass. The central part of the dyke has been flattened and the eastern end only survives as a shallow ditch The South Dyke is not as well sited for defence as the Ridge and Becca Banks on the north side of the Cock Beck and may have been replaced by the Rein which overlies it. The dating evidence shows a prehistoric date for the construction of the ditch with a Roman redefinition and filling in around the third century AD.
References:
Alcock
Ordnance Survey
Roberts I & Berg

Wiltshire

The Bedwyn Dyke
Unknown

The Bedwyn Dyke starts below Chisbury Hillfort and is 2.4 km long. The dyke faces north. It is comparable in size to the East Wansdyke; together the width of bank and ditch is 17.8 m. Hosttetter and Howe estimate the height of the dyke to be about 3–4 m originally and 7–8 m wide. There is some slight evidence for a counterscarp bank but most areas too badly damaged by ploughing to be certain. Fox & Fox link the dyke with Cissa of Wessex. Hosttetter & Howe question the idea of a Bedwyn Dyke 'system' and suggest it was a Roman villa estate boundary.
References:
Fox & Fox
Hostetter & Howe

East Wansdyke
Post-Roman

The east Wansdyke runs from Morgan's Hill to Savernake Forest and is 21 km long. The width of bank and ditch is up to 28 m wide. The east Wansdyke is much smaller at the eastern end on clay soil. A counterscarp bank exists for some parts of the East Wansdyke. The Wansdyke enters Savernake Forest and stops. The eastern end of the Wansdyke, in the West Woods of Overton and Fyfield parishes, is unfinished with only 4.5 km of dyke in the woods. In these woods the Wansdyke is made of a series of dumps, 0.5 to 0.75 m high.

References:

P. J. Fowler, 'Landscape Plotted and Pieced: landscape history and local archaeology in Fyfield and Overton Wiltshire'

P. Fowler

Fox & Fox

H. S. Green

Ordnance Survey

SCOTLAND

Dumfries and Galloway

The Deil's Dyke

Unknown

The Deil's Dyke consists of a bank 2–4 m wide and up to 0.7 m high with an intermittent ditch of 0.5 m wide and 0.4 m deep on the uphill side. It seems to be built to separate arable land from pasture and changes direction frequently to enclose as much land as possible. It is unlikely to be a political boundary and is certainly not the massive political boundary all around Galloway that Train believed.

References:

Barber

Graham, 'The Deil's Dyke in Galloway'

Graham & Feachem, 'The Deil's Dyke in Dumfriesshire and Ayrshire'

The Scottish Borders

The Catrail

Unknown

The Catrail is also known as the Picts' Work Ditch. The Catrail is uncertain for part of its course, badly damaged by ploughing and forestry. It possibly links a number of hillforts in the Borders. It may have functioned as a large scale territorial boundary. Antiquarians tried to extend it to link up with monuments such as the Black Dykes in Northumberland and the Scot's Dyke in Yorkshire.

References:

Barber

F. Lynn

WALES

Carmarthenshire

Clwadd Mawr

Unknown

A substantial monument in Carmarthenshire, the bank is 19 m wide and the ditch 15 m wide. The dyke runs north to south for about 1.5 km. Each end of the dyke stands on a steep-sided valley. The dyke runs parallel to the modern road between Carmarthen and Newcastle Emlyn. This is possibly on the line of a Roman road. The ditch is on the eastern side so the dyke faces eastward. It has been suggested that it was a frontier line, possibly the boundary of the kingdom of Dyfed, but could also be prehistoric. There is no evidence to date this dyke. Clwadd Mawr is Welsh for the 'Big Ditch'. Without more evidence dating of the dyke is impossible and it could range from prehistoric to medieval in date. It should not be confused with the Clwadd Mawr in Powys, one of the Short Dykes.
References:
E. G. Bowen
Ordnance Survey

Powys
(Not all of the Short Dykes are included in this list.)

Clawdd Mawr Dyke

Post-Roman

The dyke is about 450 m long and bank 1.6 m high with a ditch on the north side, 1.8 m deep, except for a stretch where there is a ditch on the south side as well. Radiocarbon dating of the dyke gave an age of Cal AD 630–710 as part of the Short Dykes project.
References:
Hankinson &Caseldine

Crugyn Bank Dyke

Post-Roman

The Crugyn Bank Dyke is in the extreme south of the old county of Montgomeryshire and also known as The Double Dyche. It is at least 470 m long but possibly longer. The bank is 1.2 m high and there is a counterscarp 0.6 m in front of the bank. Dated as part of the Short Dykes project it gave a radiocarbon date of Cal AD 650–780.
References:
Hankinson & Caseldine

Giant's Grave Dyke
Post-Roman

This is a bivallate dyke with a ditch between two banks. It is about 240 m long with the bank on the east side 0.8m high and 6 m wide and the west bank is 0.3 m high and 4m wide. The ditch is 2–3 m wide and 0.4 m deep. The radiocarbon date obtained by the Short Dykes project was Cal AD 340–530. This is earlier than the dates for the other dykes but was done on peat, not charcoal.
References:
Hankinson & Caseldine

Lower Short Ditch
Post-Roman
See under Shropshire.

Offa's Dyke
Post-Roman

There are four sections of Offa's Dyke in Powys as the line of the dyke does not follow the English–Welsh border.
References:
C. Fox, *Offa's Dyke*
Hill, 'Offa's & Wat's Dykes'
Ordnance Survey

Upper Short Ditch
Post-Roman

The Upper Short Ditch straddles the border between Shropshire and Powys and England and Wales. Excavation has shown a rock cut ditch. The scheduled part of the dyke is 230 m but is at least 550 m long. Bank is 3 m high at maximum. The radiocarbon date obtained by the Short Dykes project was Cal AD 540–660.
References:
Hankinson & Caseldine

Wantyn Dyke
Unknown

The Wantyn Dyke lies 3 km to the east of the village of Kerry. The dyke is about 3 km long. It is also spelt as Wanten Dyke. Included as one of the Welsh Short Dykes by Fox but has not been dated.
References:
C. Fox, *Offa's Dyke*

Wrexham

Offa's Dyke

Offa's Dyke in Wrexham follows the higher ground from Chirk via Ruabon where it comes close to Wat's Dyke to cross into Flintshire at Brymbo.

References:

C. Fox, *Offa's Dyke*

Hill, 'Offa's & Wat's Dykes'

Ordnance Survey

Wat's Dyke

Wat's Dyke runs through Wrexham from Chirk past the town of Wrexham to cross into Flintshire.

References:

C. Fox, *Offa's Dyke*

Hill, 'Offa's & Wat's Dykes'

Ordnance Survey

Denbighshire

Offa's Dyke

Here is possibly the northern extension of Offa's Dyke. See the entry on the Whitford Dyke under Flintshire.

References:

C. Fox, *Offa's Dyke*

Hill, 'Offas & Wat's Dykes'

Ordnance Survey

Whitford Dyke

Unknown

The Whitford Dyke covers Denbighshire and Flintshire. See the entry under Flintshire.

Flintshire

Offa's Dyke

Offa's Dyke in Flintshire runs from the border with Wrexham to the agreed end at Treuddyn. See Whitford Dyke entry for the earthwork that may be a continuation of Offa's Dyke.

References:

C. Fox, *Offa's Dyke*

Hill, 'Offa's & Wat's Dykes'
Ordnance Survey

Wat's Dyke

Wat's Dyke runs through Flintshire to Coed-Llys where it stops as a continuous earthwork. The are traces of the dyke at Holywell on the coast.
References:
C. Fox, *Offa's Dyke*
Hill, 'Offa's & Wat's Dykes'
Ordnance Survey

Whitford Dyke

Unknown
The Whitford Dyke was regarded by Fox a part of Offa's Dyke, part of the northern extension beyond Treuddyn while Hill & Worthington believe it is a medieval boundary unconnected with Offa's Dyke.
References:
C. Fox, *Offa's Dyke*
Hill & Worthington, *Offa's Dyke History and Guide*

BIBLIOGRAPHY

Alcock, L., 'Aberford Dykes: the first defence of the Brigantes?' *Antiquity* 28 (1954): pp. 147–154.

Andersen, H. H., 'Danewerk' in Jankuhn, Herbert & Heinrich Beck, *Reallexikon der Germanischen Altertumskunde*, Vol. 5 (1973).

Andresen, Jens, Rasmus Iversen and Peter Jensen, 'On the War-path: Terestrial Military Organisation in Prehistoric Denmark.' *CAA proceedings Berlin* (n.d.).

Ashbee, P., 'Excavation in the "Roman Rig" near Wentworth in South-West Yorkshire.' *Transactions of the Hunter Archaeological Society* 7 (1956): pp. 256–65.

Asser, *Alfred the Great: Asser's 'Life of King Alfred' and Other Contemporary Sources*. Trans. Simon Keynes. Penguin (2004).

Astill, G. G., 'Excavations at Grim's Bank Aldermaston 1978.' *Berkshire Archaeological Journal* 70 (1979): pp. 57–65.

Babington, Charles C., 'On the foss, or devil's ditch, near Brandon, and that near Swaffham in the county of Norfolk.' *Proceedings of the Cambridge Antiquarian Society* 1 (n.d.): pp. 95–96.

Baillie, M. G., and D. M. Brown, 'Further dates from the Dorsey.' *Emania Bulletin of the Navan Research Group* 6 (1989): p. 11.

Bapty, Ian, 'The Final Word On Offa's Dyke?' *The Clwyd-Powys Archaeological Trust*, 01 May 2010 http://www.cpat.org.uk/offa/offrev.htm.

Barber, J., 'The Linear Earthworks of Southern Scotland, survey and classification.' *Transactions of the Dumfriesshire and Galloway Natural History and Antiquarian Society* 73 (1999): pp. 79–110.

Bardon, Jonathan, *A History of Ulster*. Belfast (1992).

Bassett, Steven, *The Origins of Anglo-Saxon Kingdoms*. Leicester University Press (1989).

Bedwin, Owen, and Chris Place, 'Late Iron Age and Romano-British occupation at Ounces Barn, Boxgrove, West Sussex; excavations 1982–83.' *Sussex Archaeological Collections* 133 (1995): pp. 45–101.

Bedwin, Owen, 'Excavations at the Devil's Ditch, Boxgrove, West Sussex 1981.' *Sussex Archaeological Collections* 120 (1982): pp. 37–43.

Beldam, J., 'Untitled.' *Archaeological Journal* XXV (1868).

Biddle, M, et al., *The future of London's past : a survey of the archaeological implications of planning and development in the nation's capital.* Rescue (1973).

Blair, John, 'Frithuwold's Kingdom and the origin of Surrey.' In Basset, Simon, *The Origin of Anglo-Saxon Kingdoms.* Leicester: Leicester University Press (1989).

Boldrini, N., 'Creating space: a re-examination of the Roman ridge.' *Transactions of the Hunter Archaeological Society* 20 (1999): pp. 24–30.

Boon, George C., 'The Latest Objects from Silchester, Hants.' *Medieval Archaeology* 3 (1959): pp. 79–88.

—, 'The Roman Town Calleva Atrebatum at Silchester Hampshire.' Reading Museum & Art Gallery (1972).

Bowen, E. G., 'Clawdd Mawr Carmarthenshire.' *Bulletin of the Board of Celtic Studies* 15 (1937): pp. 383–85.

Bowen, H. C., *The Archaeology of Bokerley Dyke.* RCHME (1990).

Bowlt, Colin, 'A possible extension to Grim's Dyke.' In Clark, John. *Londinium and Beyond* Vol. 156. Council for British Archaeology (2008).

Bradley, R., 'Stock raising and the origins of the hillfort on the South Downs.' *Antiquaries Journal* (1971): pp. 8–29.

—, 'The South Oxfordshire Grim's Ditch and its significance.' *Oxoniensia* 33 (1969): pp. 1–13.

Bradley, Richard, 'A Field Survey of the Chichester Entrenchments.' In Cunliffe, *Excavations at Fishbourne 1961–1969, Vol 1: The Site.* The Society of Antiquaries of London Research Reports 26 (1971).

Bradley, S. A. J., *Anglo-Saxon poetry.* London: Dent (1982).

Braun, H. S., 'Some Earthworks of North-West Middlesex.' *London and Middlesex Archaeological Society Transactions* 7 (1937): pp. 365–92.

Breeze, D., and B. Dobson, *Hadrian's Wall.* Penguin (1978).

Brewer, J. Norris, *The beauties of England and Wales Introduction to the original delineations, topographical, historical, and descriptive.* London (1818).

Brooks, Nicholas, 'The formation of the Mercian Kingdom.' In Basset, Steven, *The Origin of Anglo-Saxon Kingdoms.* Leicester University Press (1989).

Bryson, Bill, *Notes from a Small Island.* Black Swan (1995).

Burleigh, Gil, 'The Mile Ditches near Royston: Excavations 1978.' *Hertfordshire's Past* 8 (1980): pp. 25–29.

Caesar, *The Conquest of Gaul.* Trans. S. A. Handford. Penguin Classics (1951).

Castle, Stephen A., 'Excavations in Pear Wood, Brockley Hill Middlesex 1948 – 1973.' *London and Middlesex Archaeological Society Transactions* 26 (1975): pp. 267–77.

Christensen, L., 'Olgerdiget.' In Jankuhn, Herbert and Heinrich Beck, *Reallexikon der Germanischen Altertumskunde* (1973).

Clarke, R. Rainbird, 'The Fossditch a linear earthwork in southwest Norfolk.' Norfolk *Archaeology* 31 (1955): pp. 178–96.

Clarkson, Christopher, *The history of Richmond in the county of York* (1814).

Clifford, E. M., 'The Earthworks at Rodborough, Amberley and Minchinhampton.' *Transactions of the Bristol and Gloucestershire Archaeological Society* 59 (1937): pp. 287–307.

Cockin, Guy, 'Grim's Bank, Aldermaston, Berkshire (SU 611639).' *CBA Wessex News April 2006* (2006).

Coe, Duncan, and John W. Hawkes, 'Field survey and excavation on Worgret Heath, 1990.' *Dorset Natural History and Archaeological Society Proceedings* 113 (1991): pp. 33–40.

Coffin, S., 'Linear Earthworks in the Froxfield East Tisted and Hayling Wood District.' *Proceedings of the Hampshire Field Club* 32 (1975): pp. 77–81.

Copeland, Y., 'The North Oxfordshire Grim's Ditch: A fieldwork survey.' *Oxoniensia* 53 (1988): pp. 277–92.

Crawford, O. G. S., *Archaeology in the Field* (1953).

—, 'Grim's Ditch in Wychwood Oxon.' *Antiquity* 4.15 (1930): pp. 303–15.

—, *Said and done: the autobiography of an archaeologist.* Weidenfeld & Nicolson (1955).

Crawford, O. G. S., *The Andover District.* OUP (1922).

—, 'The Chiltern Grim's Ditches.' *Antiquity* 5 (1931): pp. 161–70.

—, 'The Mile Ditches at Royston.' *Antiquity* 8 (1934): pp. 216–22.

—, 'The Work of Giants.' *Antiquity* 10 (1936): pp. 173–74.

Cronk, K. A., *Journey Along the roman Ridge: Exploring the Purpose of South-West Yorkshire's Ancient Dykes.* The Clifton & Wellgate Local History Group (2004).

—, *South West Yorkshire's Roman Ridge: A Who-dug-it Mystery.* The Clifton & Wellgate Local History Group (2004).

Crow, J. G., 'The Function of Hadrian's Wall and the Comparative Evidence of Late Roman Long Walls.' *Studien zu den Militiirgrenzen Roms III. 13. internationaler Limeskongreß 3, Aalen 1983* (1986): pp. 724–29.

Currie, C. R. J., et al., 'A History of the County of Gloucestershire.' Victoria County History (1996). Accessed 31 May 2010 <http://www.british-history.ac.uk/report.aspx?compid=23262>

Dark, K., *Britain and the end of the Roman Empire.* Tempus (2000).

Davies, O., 'Excavations on the Dorsey and Black Pig's Dyke.' *Ulster Journal of Archaeology* 3 (1940): pp. 31–37.

—, 'The Black Pig's Dyke.' *Ulster Journal of Archaeology* 18 (1955): pp. 29–36.

Davis, J., 'Grim's Ditch in Buckinghamshire and Hertfordshire.' *Records of Buckinghamshire* 23 (1981): pp. 23–31.

de la Bédoyère, Guy, *The Golden Age of Roman Britain.* Stroud: Tempus (1999).

Dickens, Charles, 'Joseph Train.' *Household Words* 173 (1853): pp. 475–76.

Dyer, J. F., 'Dray's Ditches, Bedfordshire, and early Iron Age territorial boundaries in the eastern Chilterns.' *Antiquaries Journal* 41 (1961): pp.44–62.

Dyer, J., *Southern England: An Archaeological Guide* (1973).

—, 'The Chiltern Grim's Ditch.' *Antiquity* 37 (1963): pp. 46–53.

Ellis, R., 'Excavations at Grim's Dyke, Harrow, 1979.' *Transactions of the London and Middlesex Archaeological Society* 33 (1982): pp. 173–76.

English Heritage, 'Monument Class Description – Cross – Dykes.' English Heritage (January 1990). Accessed 1 July 2009 <http://www.eng-h.gov.uk/mpp/mcd/crossd.htm>

—, 'Monument Class Description – Linear Boundaries (Prehistoric).' English Heritage (June 1990). Accessed 1 July 2009 <http://www.eng-h.gov.uk/mpp/mcd/linb.htm>

Erskine, J. G., 'The West Wansdyke: an appraisal of the dating, dimension and construction techniques in the light of excavated evidence.' *Archaeological Journal* 164 (2007): pp. 80–108.

Esmonde Cleary, A. S., *The Ending of Roman Britain*. Batsford (1989).

Faulkner, N., *The Decline and Fall of Roman Britain*. Tempus (2000).

Ferns, J. L., 'The Dykes: Three big errors in History Books.' *The Historian* 9 (1985): pp. 13–14.

Fine, D., 'An Excavation of the North Oxfordshire Grim's Ditch at North Leigh.' *Oxoniensia* 41 (1977): pp. 12–16.

Fitzpatrick-Matthews, Keith J., 'Wat's Dyke: a North Welsh linear boundary.' *Wansdyke Project 21* (2001). Accessed 20 May 2010 <http://www.wansdyke21.org.uk/wansdyke/wanart/matthews1.htm>

Ford, S., 'Field work and excavation on the Berkshire Grims Ditch.' *Oxoniensia* 47 (1982): pp. 13–36.

—, 'Linear earthworks on the Berkshire Downs.' *Berkshire Archaeological Journal* 71 (1983): pp. 1–21.

Fowler, P. J., 'Cross Dykes on the Ebble-Nadder Ridge.' *Wiltshire Archaeological and Natural History Magazine* 59 (1964): pp. 46–57.

—, 'Interim Report on an Excavation in Combs Ditch Dorset, 1964.' *Dorset Natural History and Archaeological Society Proceedings* 86 (1964): p. 112.

—, *Landscape Plotted and Pieced: landscape history and local archaeology in Fyfield and Overton Wiltshire*. Society of Antiquaries of London (2000).

Fowler, Peter, 'Wansdyke in the Woods.' In Ellis, Peter, *Roman Wiltshire and After*. Wiltshire Archaeological and Natural History Society (2001): pp. 179–98.

Fox, C., and A. Fox, 'Wansdyke reconsidered.' *Archaeological Journal* 115 (1958): pp. 1–48.

Fox, Cyril, and M. Palmer W., 'Excavations at the Fleam Dyke and at Foxton.' *Proceedings of the Cambridge Antiquarian Society* 25 (1922): pp. 21–46.

Fox, Cyril, *Offa's Dyke*. London: The British Academy (1955).

—, *The archaeology of the Cambridge region*. Cambridge Univeristy Press (1923).

—, *The Personality of Britain*. Cardiff: National Museum of Wales (1943).

Fox, Cyril, B. H. St J., O'Neil, and W. F. Grimes, 'Linear Earthworks; Methods of Field Survey.' *Antiquaries Journals* 26 (1946): pp. 175–79.

Frere, S. S., 'British Urban Defences in Earthwork.' *Britannia* 15 (1984).

Gardiner, K. S., 'The Wansdyke Diktat? a discussion paper.' *Bristol and Avon Archaeology* 15 (1998): pp. 57–65.

Gildas, *The Ruin of Britain and other documents*. Philmore (1978).

Godsal, Major P., *Woden's, Grim's and Offa's Dykes* (1913).

Goldsmith, J., *The Natural and Artifical Wonders of the United Kingdom*. London (1825).

Graham, Angus, and R. W. Feachem, 'The Deil's Dyke in Dumfriesshire and Ayrshire.' *Proceedings of the Society of Anquaries of Scotland* 88 (1956): pp. 137–54.

Graham, Angus, 'The Deil's Dyke in Galloway.' *Proceedings of the Society of Anquaries of Scotland* 83 (1949): pp.174–85.

Green, D., and L. F. Preston, 'Two Excavations in the 'Roman Ridge' Dyke.' *Transactions of the Hunter Archaeological Society* 7 (1951): pp. 20–25.

Green, D., 'The Roman Ridge Hill Top, Kimberworth near Rotherham.' *Transactions of the Hunter Archaeological Society* 6 (1947): pp. 95–97.

Green, H. S., 'Wansdyke excavations, 1966 to 1970.' *Wiltshire Archaeological and Natural History Magazine* 66 (1971): pp. 129–46.

Grigg, Erik, 'Dark Age Dykes.' *Wansdyke Project* 21 (2006). Accessed 8 July 2009 <http://www.wansdyke21.org.uk/wansdyke/wanart/grigg.htm>

Grinsell, L. V., *The Archaeology of Wessex* (1957).

Guest, Edwin, *Origines celticae (a fragment) and other contributions to the history of Britain*. Ed. William Stubbs and Cecil Deedes. London: Macmillan & Co. (1883).

Guilbert, G., 'Ratlinghope/Sitt Hill, Shropshire: earthwork enclosures and cross-dykes.' *Bulletin of the Board of Celtic Studies* 26 (1975): pp. 363–73.

Halpin, Eoin, 'The Devil's Dyke II, Nithsdale.' *Transactions of the Dumfriesshire and Galloway Natural History and Antiquarian Society* 59 (1984): pp. 27–32.

Hankinson, R., and A. Caseldine, 'Short Dykes in Powys and their Origins.' *The Archaeological Journal* 163 (2006): pp. 266–69.

Hannaford, H. R., 'An excavation on Wat's Dyke at Mile Oak, Oswestry, Shropshire.' *Shropshire History and Archaeology* 73 (1998): pp. 1–7.

Harrison, S., 'The Icknield Way: Some Queries.' *The Archaeological Journal* 160 (2003): pp. 1–22.

Hart, C. R., *The North Derbyshire Archaeological Survey to AD 1500* (1981).

Hawkes, C. F., 'Bokerley Dyke and Woodyates.' *Antiquaries Journal* 54 (1947): pp. 62–78.

Hawkes, C. F. C., and M. R. Hull, *Camulodunum*. London: Society of Antiquaries of London (1947).

Hawkes, C. F. C., and Philip Crummy, *Colchester Archaeological Report 11: Camulodunum 2*. Colchester Archaeological Trust Ltd (1995).

Hayes, Laurence, and Timothy Malim, 'The Date and Nature of Wat's Dyke: a Reassessment in the Light of Recent Investigations at Gobowen, Shropshire.' *Anglo-Saxon Studies in Archaeology and History* 15 (2008): pp. 147–79.

Heather, Peter, *The Goths*. Blackwell, 1996.

Hill, D., and M. Worthington, *Offa's Dyke History and Guide*. Tempus Publishing (2003).

Hill, D., 'Offas & Wat's Dykes.' *Transactions of Lancashire and Cheshire Archaeological Society* 79 (1977): pp. 21–23.

Hillson, W. W., 'The earthwork on Morden Bog, Wareham, Dorset 1972 (10th year) – 1990 (27th year).' In Bell, M, P. J. Fowler, and S. W. Hillson, *The Experimental Earthwork Project 1960 – 1992.* CBA (1996).

Hogg, A. H., 'Dyke on Hartford Bridge Flats.' *Proceedings of the Hampshire Field Club* 13 (1935): pp. 70–74.

Hogg, H. A., 'Earthworks in Joydens Wood, Bexley, Kent.' *Archaeologia Cantiana* 54 (1940): pp. 10–27.

Hope-Taylor, Brian, and David Hill, 'The Cambridgeshire Dykes: I, the Devil's Dyke investigations, 1973; II, Bran Ditch – the burials reconsidered.' *Proceedings of the Cambridge Antiquarian Society* 66 (1976): pp. 123–28.

Hostetter, E., and T. N. Howe, 'Observations on the Bedwyn Dyke.' *The Romano-British Villa at Castle Copse, Great Bedwyn* (n.d.).

Hughes, Michael W., 'Grimsditch and Cuthwulf's Expedition to the Chilterns in AD 571.' *Antiquity* 5 (1931): pp. 291–314.

Hunn, J. R., 'The earthworks of Prae Wood [Hertfordshire]: an interim account.' *Britannia* 11 (1980): pp. 21–30.

Huntingdon, Henry of, *Historia Anglorum: the history of the English people.* Trans. Diana E. Greenway. OUP (1996).

Iles, R., 'West Wansdyke: recent archaeological research and future prospects.' *Bristol and Avon Archaeology* 7 (1988): pp. 6–10.

Irving, G. V., 'Notes of an examination of the Devil's Dyke in Dumfriesshire.' *Proceedings of the Society of Anquaries of Scotland* 5 (1862): pp. 189–195.

Johnson, N. D., 'The Bolster Bank a Survey.' *Cornish Archaeology* 19 (1980): pp. 77–88.

Kane, W. F., 'Additional Researches on the Black Pig's Dyke.' *Proceedings of the Royal Irish Academy* 33 (1917): pp. 539–63.

—, 'The black pig's dyke: the ancient boundary fortification of Uladh.' *Proceedings of the Royal Irish Academy* 27 (1909): pp. 301–28.

Karloukovski, Vassil, and Mark W. Hounslow, *Report on the archaeomagnetic dating of a sediment fill from Scots' Dyke, Scotch Corner, North Yorkshire.* Centre for Environmental Magnetism and Palaeomagnetism. Lancaster: Centre for Environmental Magnetism and Palaeomagnetism (CEMP) Geography Dept, Lancaster Environment Centre, Lancaster University (2006).

Knudsen, Aage Svend, and Per Ole Rindel, 'Trældiget' (n.d.).

Laycock, S., *Britannia the failed state.* Tempus (2008).

Leland, John, *The Itinerary of John Leland.* Ed. L. S. Smith. Centaur Press (1964).

Lethbridge, T. C., 'The Car Dyke, the Cambridgeshire Ditches and the Anglo-Saxons.' *Proceedings of the Cambridge Antiquarian Society* 35 (1934): pp. 90–96.

—, 'The riddle of the Dykes.' *Proceedings of the Cambridge Antiquarian Society* 51 (1958).

Lynn, C. J., 'Excavations at the Dorsey, County Armagh, 1977.' *Ulster Journal of Archaeology* 54–5 (1992): pp. 61–77.

—, 'The Dorsey and other linear earthworks.' *Studies on early Ireland : Essays in honour of M. V. Duignan* (1982): pp. 121–28.

Lynn, F., 'A survey of the Catrail.' *Proceedings of the Society of Antiquaries of Scotland* 32 (1898): pp. 78–79.

Mack, J. L., 'The Old Scots Dike: its construction, AD 1552, and its destruction, 1917–1920.' *Transactions of the Hawick Archaeological Society* (1923): pp. 3–5.

Malim, T., 'New evidence on the Cambridgeshire Dykes and Warstead Street Roman Road.' *Proceedings of the Cambridge Antiquarian Society* 80 (1996): pp. 27–122.

—, 'The Origins and Design of Linear Earthworks in the Welsh Marches.' *Landscape Enquiries the proceedings of the Clifton Archaeological Club* 8 (2007): pp. 13–32.

Marcellinus, Ammianus, *Roman History*. Trans. J. C. Rolfe. Loeb Classics (n.d.).

Merrifield, Ralph, *London City of the Romans*. Batsford (1983).

Mikkelsen, Poul, and Lis Helles Olesen, 'Vendeldiget.' *KUML* (1996): pp. 135–47.

Nielsen, Ann-Lili, '*Götavirke : en omdiskuterad vallanläggning.*' In *Människors platser: tretton arkeologiska studier från UV* (2000).

Nithard, *Carolingian chronicles: Royal Frankish annals and Nithard's Histories.* University of Michigan Press (1972).

Northern Archaeological Associates, 'A66 Improvements Archaeological Trial Trenching Carkin Moor to Scots Corner North Yorkshire Final Report.' Unpublished Report (2000).

—, 'A66 Upgrading to dual carriageway Stage 2 Archaeological Assesment Area A Scotch Corner to Greta Bridge' (1997).

O'Neil, B. H., and H. E. Peake, 'A Linear Earthwork on Greenham Common Berkshire.' *The Archaeological Journal* 50 (1943): pp. 177–87.

O'Neil, B. H., 'Grey Ditch, Bradwell, Derbyshire.' *Antiquity* 19 (1945): p. 119.

—, 'Grim's Bank Padworth Berkshire.' *Antiquity* 17 (1943): pp. 188–95.

—, 'The Silchester Region in the 5th & 6th centuries AD.' *Antiquity* 17 (1944): pp. 113–23.

Ordnance Survey, *Britain in the Dark Ages. North sheet map.* Southampton: Director General, at the Ordnance Survey Office (1939).

—, *Britain in the Dark Ages. South sheet map.* Southampton: Southampton: First published by the Director General, at the Ordnance Survey Office (1935).

—, *Map of Britain in the Dark Ages.* Southampton: Ordnance Survey (1971).

Oxford Archaeology North, 'A66 (Package A), Road Improvement Scheme Greta Bridge to Scotch Corner Archaeological Post-excavation Assessment' (2008).

Page, William, ed., *The Victoria history of the county of Cornwall.* St Catherine Press, 1906.

Piggot, C. M., 'The Grim's Ditch complex in Cramborne Chase.' *Antiquity* 18 (1944): pp. 65–71.

Pitt Rivers, A. H., and L. Fox, *Excavations in Bokerly and Wansdyke Dorset and Wilts 1888–1891.* Privately printed (1892).

—, 'On Excavations in the Earthwork Called Dane's Dyke at Flamborough in October, 1879; and on the Earthworks of the Yorkshire Wolds.' *The Journal of the Anthropological Institute of Great Britain and Ireland* 11 (1882): pp. 455–71.

Preston, F. L., 'A Field Survey of the Roman Rig Dyke in SW Yorkshire.' *Transactions of the Hunter Archaeological Society* 6 (1949): pp. 197–220.

Pryor, F., *Britain AD: A Quest for Arthur, England and the Anglo-Saxons.* HarperCollins (2004).

Rahtz, P. A., 'An excavation on Bokerly Dyke 1958.' *Antiquaries Journal* 68 (1961): pp. 65–99.

Rahtz, P., 'Anglo-Saxon Yorkshire: Current Research Problems.' In Geake, H., and J. Kenny, *Early Deira: Archaeological Studies of the East Riding in the Fourth to Ninth Centuries AD.* Oxford: Oxbow Books (2000).

Ramm, H. G., 'Roman Roads west of Tadcaster.' *York Historian* 1 (1976).

Reid, B., 'The Minchinhampton Bulwarks: A Post-Roman Frontier.' *Glevensis* 32 (2000): pp. 3–9.

Riley, D. N., 'Investigation of Entrance through "Roman Ridge" in Shepard's Plantation, Greasborough nr Rotherham.' *Transactions of the Hunter Archaeological Society* 7 (1951): pp. 18–19.

Roberts I., Burgess A., and D. Berg, *A New Link to the Past: The Archaeological Landscape of the M1-A1 Link Road.* West Riding Archaeological Service (2001).

Rodd, Lord Rennel, 'Note on the Rowe Ditch and an "second" alignment of Offa's Dyke in the Pembridge – Wapley – Herrock area.' *Transactions of the Radnorshire Society* 30 (1960): p. 31.

Royal Commission on Historical Monuments (England), *An inventory of historical monuments in the County of Cambridgeshire Volume 2 north-east Cambridgeshire.* HMSO (1972).

—, *Iron Age and Romano-British Monuments in the Gloucestershire Cotswolds.* London: HMSO (1976).

Sauer, Eberhard W., *Linear Earthwork, Tribal Boundary and Ritual Beheading: Aves Ditch from the Iron Age to the Early Middle Ages.* BAR Archaeopress (2005).

Sherratt, Andrew, 'Why Wessex? The Avon route and river transport in later British Prehistory.' *Oxford Journal of Archaeology* 15.2 (1996): pp. 211–34.

Smith, E., 'Scots Dike Earthwork North Yorkshire.' Final project for Certificate in archaeology at University of Durham (1990).

Spain, G. R., 'The Black Dyke in Northumberland.' *Archaeologica Aeliana* 19 (1922): pp. 121–68.

Stenton, Frank, *Anglo-Saxon England.* Oxford University Press (1971).

Stone, H. J., 'The Pinner Grim's Dyke.' *London and Middlesex Archaeological Society Transactions* 7 (1937): 284–301.

Stukeley, William, *Stonehenge, a temple restor'd to the British Druids.* Forgotten Books, 2007.

Sumner, H., 'Comb's Ditch and Bokerly Dyke Reviewed.' *Dorset Natural History and Archaeological Society Proceedings* 52 (1930): 59–74.

Tacitus, *Complete Works of Tacitus*. Random House , 1943.

—, *The Annals of Imperial Rome*. Trans. Michael Grant. Penguin, 1956.

Taylor, C., *Dorset*. 1970.

—, *Roads and tracks of Britain*. 1979.

Thompson, Isabel, 'Harrow AD 400–AD 1066.' *Two Thousand Years: The long journey*. The Stanmore and Harrow Historical Society (2000).

—, 'Harrow in the Roman Period.' *Transactions of the London and Middlesex Archaeological Society* 59 (2008): pp. 61–80.

Wade-Martins, P., 'The Linear Earthworks of West Norfolk.' *Norfolk Archaeology* 36 (1974): pp. 23–38.

Waldron, Arthur, *The Great Wall of China: From History to Myth*. Cambridge University Press (2008).

Whaley, Richard, 'Festæn Dyke and Roman Road on Hartford Bridge Flats.' *North East Hampshire Historical and Archaeological Society* 1 (2000): pp. 29–35.

Wheeler, R. E., 'London and the Grim's Ditches.' *Antiquaries Journal* 14 (1934): pp. 254–63.

Wheeler, R. E. M., and T. V. Wheeler, *Verulamium; A Belgic and two Roman cities*. Society of Antiquaries of London Report XI (1936).

Wileman, J., 'The purpose of the dykes: understanding the linear earthworks of early medieval Britain.' *Landscapes* 4 (2003): pp. 59–66.

Williams-Freeman, J. P., 'Cross-Dykes.' *Antiquity* 6 (1934): pp. 24–34.

Wilmott, T., 'Excavation and survey on the line of Grim's Ditch, West Yorkshire 1977–83.' *Yorkshire Archaeological Journal* 65 (1993): pp. 55–74.

Wood, Michael, *In Search of the Dark Ages*. BCA (1981).

Wooler, E., 'The Catrail.' *Proceedings of the Society of Antiquaries of Newcastle on Tyne* 2 (1905): pp. 64–76.

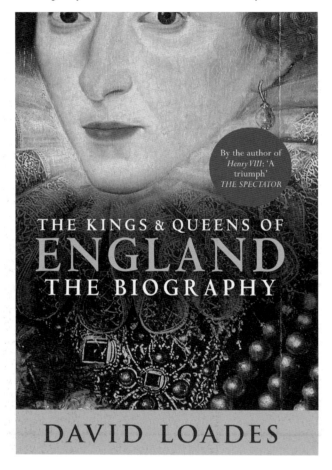

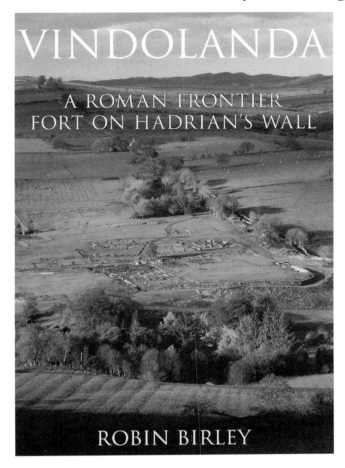

Also available from Amberley Publishing

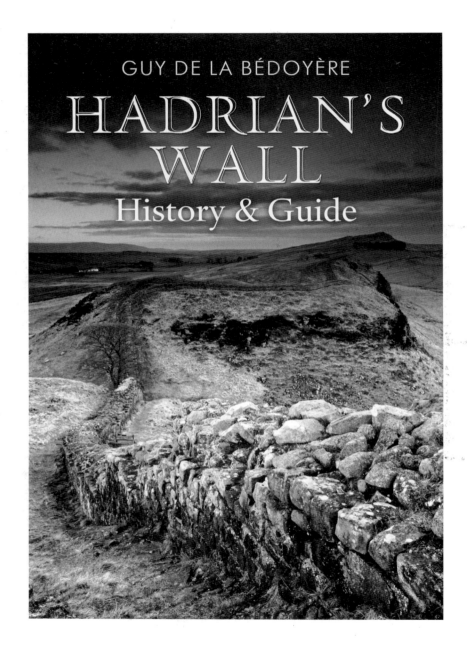